JB JOSSEY-BASS

HANDS-ON BIBLE EXPLORATIONS

52 Fun Activities for Christian Learning

Janice VanCleave

BICENTENNIAL
1807
WILEY
2007
BICENTENNIAL

John Wiley & Sons, Inc.

Published by John Wiley & Sons, Inc., Hoboken, New Jersey
Published simultaneously in Canada

Design and composition by Navta Associates, Inc.

For general information about our other products and services, please contact our Customer Care Department within the United States at (800) 762-2974, outside the United States at (317) 572-3993 or fax (317) 572-4002.

Wiley also publishes its books in a variety of electronic formats. Some content that appears in print may not be available in electronic books. For more information about Wiley products, visit our web site at www.wiley.com.

Library of Congress Cataloging-in-Publication Data:

VanCleave, Janice Pratt.
    Hands-on Bible explorations : 52 fun activities for Christian learning / Janice VanCleave
        p. cm.
    Includes index.
    ISBN-13 978-0-471-47201-8 (pbk.)
    ISBN-10 0-471-47201-8 (pbk.)
  1. Christian education of children. 2. Church work with children. I. Title.
    BV1471.3.v36 2006
    268'.432—dc22

                                                                        2005011808

Printed in the United States of America

10 9 8 7 6 5 4 3 2 1

CONTENTS

DEDICATION

This book is dedicated to an awesome Bible teacher who inspires his students to seek the truth of God's Word for themselves. To my friend and mentor, Dwayne Fitte.

ACKNOWLEDGMENTS

A special note of love and appreciation to Wade, the helpmate designed especially for me by God.

My thanks to the following kids from First Baptist Church in Riesel, Texas, for their help in testing the activities in this book: Kasi and Kristi Braziel, Hudson Burkart, Curt and Morgan Evans, Anthony and Austin Lee, Starla Lehrmann, Tayler and McKenzie Lowrey, Derreck Maxey, Klynt Mynar, Rebekah and William Robert, and Jacob Stanford.

A thank-you is also expressed to Tammy, Kendra, and Breanna Kleine. These special friends in Christ read the experiments in this book and gave many helpful suggestions.

I would also like to express my appreciation to my family for their unfailing support. Your input and ideas are evident throughout this book: Calvin, Ginger, Lauren, and Lacey Russell; Russell, Ginger, and David VanCleave; Mike and Tina Ryre and Davin VanCleave; Travis, Kimberly, Tyler, and Krista Bolden; Chris, Jennifer, Christopher, and Makenzie Durbin.

Introduction

This book is full of Bible activities for children ages 6 through 12. Part I includes stories from the Old Testament, Part II includes stories from the New Testament, and Part III includes lessons about Christian values, which are beliefs and ideas based on the Bible that are important in order to live a joy-filled life.

In each chapter you will find interesting facts about a Bible story or a Christian value, as well as an activity that will help you apply the story or the value presented. While you can read the chapters and do the activities in any order, you will gain a better understanding of the Bible if you read the chapters in order.

The book is designed to help you explore the Bible. The Bible references are taken from the *Kids' Devotional Bible, New International Reader's Version*. The main goals of the book are to present Bible study in a fun way and to help you make Jesus the center of your life.

HOW TO USE THE BOOK

You can start at the beginning of the book or you can just flip through the chapters for a topic that sounds interesting. Once you've decided on an activity to try, read it through completely, then collect all the needed materials and follow all the directions carefully. There are 52 activities— one for each week of the year. The activities can be used by an individual, by families, or in a Sunday school setting.

PART

I

THE OLD TESTAMENT

1 The Heavens

In the beginning, God created the heavens and the earth.—Genesis 1:1

Topic: The creation of heaven and Earth
Bible Exploration: Genesis 1:1–31

The **Bible** is the Word of God made of 66 books: 39 in the Old Testament and 27 in the New Testament. Genesis is the first book. The first chapter of Genesis introduces **God**, the loving creator and ruler of the universe. The name **Lord**, which means the master or the one in control, is also used for God. For information about God the Father, God the Son, and God the Holy Spirit, see chapter 21, "Three in One."

Genesis describes the order of **creation** (everything that exists). God created the universe, including the heavens and the Earth. **Creating** is doing something for the first time. When you create a picture, you work with paints and paper. The **miracle** (an amazing thing that only God can do) of God's creation is that He created His own supplies out of nothing.

In the Bible, the word **heaven** is used for two places, the **sky** (the part of the universe surrounding Earth) and **God's home**, where the children of God go to be with Him forever after they die.

In the following activity, you will make a model of heaven and Earth that includes the Sun, the Earth, the Moon, and stars. You don't need to use specific distances for this model. The important thing is it will help you remember that God positioned the Earth just the right distance from the Sun so that the Sun provides the necessary amount of light and heat. If Earth were any closer to the Sun, it would be too hot for living things to survive. If it were any farther away from the Sun, it would be too cold for living things to survive. Earth's position is no accident; God put it in just the right place.

——HEAVENLY MODEL——

You Need   12-by-12-inch (30-by-30-cm) piece of white poster board
drawing compass
scissors
yellow, blue, green, and brown crayons
transparent tape
three 12-inch (30-cm) pieces of string
clothes hanger
stick-on stars

1. Using the compass, draw six circles with these diameters: two that are 5 inches (12.5 cm), two that are 3 inches (7.5 cm), and two that are 1½ inches (3.75 cm).

2. Cut out the circles.

3. Cut along a straight line from the edge to the center of each circle.

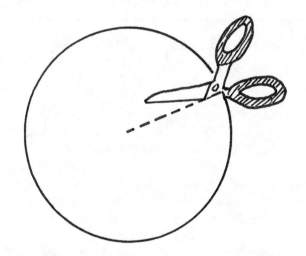

4. Use the yellow crayon to color the large circles on the front and back.

5. Fit the two large circles together and turn them so that one is on top of the other.

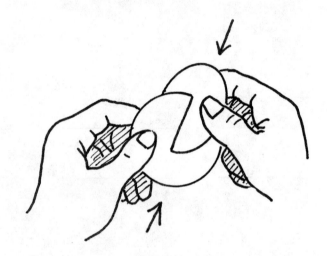

6. Tape the center edge of the stacked circles on the front and back. On one side, raise one flap and tape along the center edge as shown. Repeat on the back side.

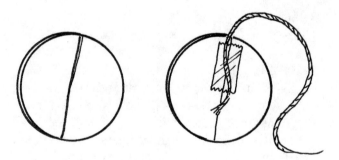

7. Tape the end of a 12-inch (30-cm) piece of string to the circle as shown.

8. Raise the flaps on the circles so that they are perpendicular (at a 90-degree angle) to each other as shown.

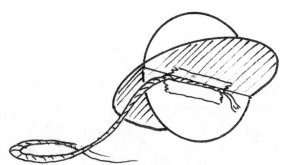

9. Use the blue crayon to color the front and back of one of the medium circles. Color the second medium circle green on one side and brown on the other. The colors represent blue for water, green for plants, and brown for land on Earth.

10. Repeat steps 5 through 8 using the medium circles to make an Earth model.

11. Repeat steps 5 through 8 using the small white circles to make a Moon model.

12. Lay the clothes hanger on a table. Tape the free ends of the strings to the clothes hanger as shown. Adjust the length of the strings so that the Earth is in line with the Sun, and the Moon is slightly higher than the Earth.

13. Adjust the position of the models on the hanger so that the hanger balances when held by the hook. Add stick-on stars .

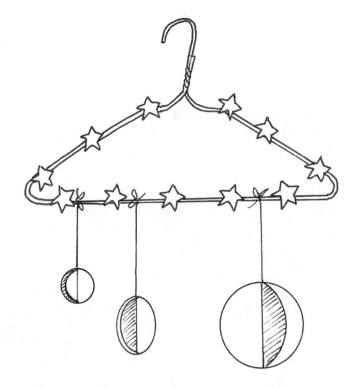

14. Hang your heavenly model in your room to remind you of how God put Earth in just the right place in the heavens.

—— Memory Verse ——

In the beginning You made the earth secure. You placed it on its foundations.
Your hands created the heavens. (Psalm 102:25)

—— Think about This ——

What are some of God's creations that you are thankful for?

2 Forbidden Fruit

The Lord God gave the man a command. He said, "You can eat the fruit of any tree that is in the garden. But you must not eat the fruit of the tree of the knowledge of good and evil."—Genesis 2:16

Topic: The results of breaking a law of God
Bible Exploration: Genesis 1:26–2:25

After God created the heavens and the Earth, He filled Earth with plants and animals. Next He formed Adam. Then He formed Eve. God prepared a beautiful place called the **Garden of Eden** for them. God had only one **law**, also called a **commandment** (a rule requiring a certain behavior), about the plants in the garden: Adam and Eve could eat from any of the plants

except the fruit from one tree. If they broke this law, the punishment would be death.

One day the **devil** (an enemy of God and people) took the form of a snake and spoke to Eve. He encouraged her to eat the fruit from the forbidden tree. The devil lied and said that Eve wouldn't die; instead, she would become wise. The devil **deceived** (tricked) Eve, and she ate the fruit. She gave some fruit to Adam, who also chose to eat it.

When Adam and Eve broke God's law by eating the forbidden fruit, they sinned. **Sin** is breaking God's laws or any action that you chose to do that doesn't honor God. Once Adam and Eve sinned, they were not innocent the way God had made them. They sinned and had a nature that would sin again. They knew they were naked and sewed fig leaves together to hide their bodies. God said they would die if they ate the forbidden fruit. While Adam's and Eve's **physical death** (death of the body) was not immediate, their **spiritual death** (separation from the fellowship of God) was. God made Adam and Eve leave the Garden of Eden because there was another tree in the garden called the "Tree of Life," and God did not want Adam and Eve to eat that tree's fruit and live forever in their sinful way.

Before Adam and Eve sinned, there was no death. The first deaths were the animals that God killed. The skins from these animals provided covering for Adam's and Eve's naked bodies as well as a covering for Adam's and Eve's sin.

The innocent animals were **sacrificed** (the killing of one thing in the place of another) for the guilty. Before Christ, animals were sacrificed for the sins of people. See chapter 34, "The Rescue Plan," for information about why animal sacrifices are no longer needed.

In the following activity, you will make two paper figures that hold hands. The figures represent Adam and Eve after they sinned. One side of the figures will be dressed in the first clothes ever worn by people and the other will be clothes made for them by God.

——ADAM AND EVE IN THE FIRST CLOTHES——

You Need   sheet of 8½-by-11-inch (21.3-by-27.5-cm) white poster board
pencil
scissors
crayons
transparent tape
ribbon

1. Fold the sheet of poster board in half so that the short edges meet.

2. Fold each short edge back toward the fold into an accordion shape.

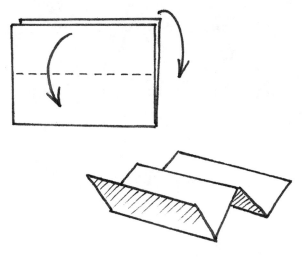

3. Use the pencil to draw one-half of a figure on one side of the folded paper (see the diagram),

taking note of the position of the folded and open edges in the diagram.

4. Cut out the half figure on the folded paper, cutting through all the layers.

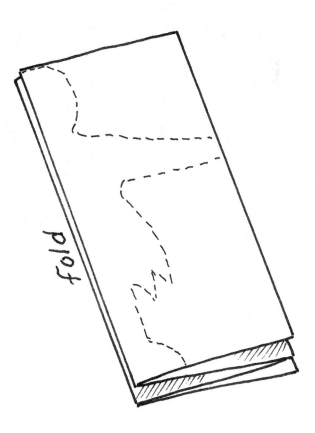

5. Unfold the paper and use crayons to draw faces, hair, and clothes on the two figures. You should draw Adam and Eve covered with clothes made of animal skins on one side and clothes made of leaves on the opposite side.

6. Tape one end of the ribbon to the head of each figure.

7. You can hang the figures in your room to remind you to follow God's rules.

front   back

— Memory Verse —

Children, obey your parents in everything.
That pleases the Lord. (Colossians 3:20)

— Think about This —

God makes rules to help and protect you. How can His rule to obey your parents help and protect you?

Rainbow Covenant

Sometimes when I bring clouds over the earth, a rainbow will appear in them. Then I will remember My covenant between Me and you and every kind of living thing. —Genesis 9:14–15

Topic: God makes an agreement with Noah
Bible Exploration: Genesis 6–9

The book of Genesis contains the story of Noah and the ark. Noah was a man who lived during a time when the people on Earth were very evil. God decided to destroy the people by causing it to rain until all the Earth was covered with water. But God chose to save Noah and told him to build an **ark,** which was a ship designed by God. The ark would save Noah and his family as well as animals that Noah put on the ark.

Noah had **faith** in God, which means he trusted and believed in God. If God said it was going to rain and flood the Earth, then it

would. Even though his neighbors laughed and made fun of him for building a boat on dry land, Noah remained **faithful** (able to be trusted and depended on) to God. When the ark was finished, Noah followed God's instructions and took his family and animals with him onto the ark. It rained and rained for 40 long days and nights. The water rose on Earth until the highest mountains were covered by more than 20 feet (6 m). Then God sent a wind to dry the water, which took about a year.

When the land was dry, God told Noah to bring his family and the animals out of the ark. God made a **covenant** with Noah and every living thing for all time. A covenant is an agreement between people or between God and people. The covenant was that God would never again destroy life on Earth by flooding it with water. God put a rainbow in the sky as a reminder of this covenant. So when dark clouds come and it rains, the rainbow is a reminder that the whole Earth will never again be flooded.

In the following activity, you will make a rainbow bookmark. Use this bookmark to remind you of God's agreement to never flood the entire Earth again.

——— RAINBOW BOOKMARK ———

You Need pencil
4-by-12-inch (10-by-30-cm) piece of white poster board
ruler
scissors
red, orange, yellow, green, blue, indigo (blue-violet), and violet crayons

1. Use the pencil to draw a cloud at one end of the piece of poster board as shown.

2. With the pencil and the ruler, draw 6 lines as evenly spaced as possible. Each line should start at the edge of the cloud.

3. Cut around the top of the cloud.

4. Use the crayons to color the stripes as shown.

5. Place your rainbow bookmark in books that you read. It will remind you that God is faithful.

red
orange
yellow
green
blue
indigo
violet

——— Memory Verse ———

I have put My rainbow in the clouds. It will be the sign of the covenant between Me and the earth. (Genesis 9:13)

——— Think about This ———

Noah built the ark and collected the animals because he had faith in God.
How do you show your faith in God?

[4] Abram Trusts God

The Lord had said to Abram, "Leave your country and your people. Leave your father's family. Go to the land I will show you."—Genesis 12:1

Topic: God's covenant with Abram
Bible Exploration: Genesis 12:1–4, 17:5

God told Abram to leave his country and relatives to travel to a land that He would show Abram. God promised Abram that he would be **blessed** (rewarded by God), his name would be great, and he would be the leader of a great nation. Abram did as the Lord asked and prepared to leave. He took his wife, Sari, his nephew, Lot, and all their possessions and workers. With God's directions they set out for the land of Canaan. God rewarded Abram as promised, and his name is known to this day.

The name **Abram** means noble father. God changed Abram's name to **Abraham**, which means father of many, because God said that Abraham would be the father of many nations.

In the following activity, you will discover that you can trust a bridge to hold you up because it has a good foundation on solid ground. If you thought about what would happen if a bridge fell, then you would be afraid to cross it. But if you think about the strong foundation of the bridge and know that it can be trusted to hold you up, then you don't have to be afraid. Abram had moments when he forgot that God could be trusted, and he became fearful. But when he remembered that God was strong and trustworthy, he was not fearful.

— OVER THE EDGE —

You Need 2 books of equal size, about 1 inch
(2.5 cm) thick
marker
11 jumbo $1\frac{1}{16}$-by-6-inch
(1.7-by-15-cm) wooden craft sticks

1. Place the books on a flat surface, such as the floor, so that they are slightly farther apart than the length of the craft sticks.

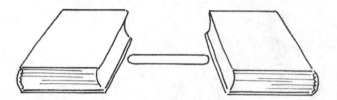

2. Use the marker to print "God" on two of the sticks (sticks 1 and 2). Place these two sticks on the books as shown. Make sure that the edges of the sticks are even with the edges of the books.

3. Place a stick on top of each stick about ½ inch (1.25 cm) past the stick on which each is laying.

This will make the top sticks (sticks 3 and 4) extend about ½ inch (1.25 cm) past the edges of the books.

4. Place another stick on top of each stack. These sticks (sticks 5 and 6) should also extend ½ inch (1.25 cm) past the sticks below them.

5. Repeat step 4 twice, first using sticks 7 and 8, then using sticks 9 and 10. There should be 5 sticks stacked on each book. One end of each stick should be over the edge of the books.

6. Carefully place the last stick (stick 11) in the middle so that it rests on each stack of sticks, but neither of its ends should be over the edges of the books.

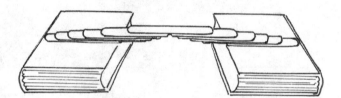

7. The last stick is supported by the two stacks of sticks below it, and the two bottom sticks form the foundation of the bridge. "God" is written on the foundation sticks to remind you that He is your foundation and that His Word, the Bible, can be trusted.

— Memory Verse —

Trust in the Lord with all your heart. Do not depend
on your own understanding. (Proverbs 3:5)

— Think about This —

You can trust God to direct you when you have problems.
How can God speak to you?

⟦5⟧ Rebekah

After she had given him a drink, she said, "I'll get water for your camels too. I'll keep doing it until they finish drinking."—Genesis 24:19

Topic: Choosing a bride for Isaac
Bible Exploration: Genesis 24:1–67

In the book of Genesis, there is a story of how a bride was selected for Isaac, Abraham's son. Abraham sent his servant to find a wife for his son. The servant was to go to Abraham's native country of Haran, where his relatives lived. Haran is also called the City of Nahor, which today is in Turkey. When the servant arrived at his destination, he made his 10 camels kneel down by a well where the women of the city drew water. He asked God to help him select one of the women who would be coming to the well.

The servant prayed that when he asked a woman to give him a drink of water, the woman whom God selected to be Isaac's bride would not only give him a drink but would also offer to give water to all of his camels until they were finished drinking. This was no small task. Camels can go for weeks without drinking, but when they do drink, they drink very large amounts. Some drink as much as 35 gallons (140 liters) of water at one time.

A girl named Rebekah gave the servant water and drew enough water for all of the camels. In this way, the servant knew that Rebekah was the bride whom God had chosen for Isaac.

In the following activity, you will make paper

sun visors that represent the natural sun visors of a camel. The camel's visors are the bones that form broad ridges that stick out above the camel's eyes. God made camels with these bones so that their eyes would be protected from the bright desert sunlight.

—— SUN VISORS ——

You Need   index card
scissors
36-inch (1-m) piece of string
transparent tape

1. Fold the index card in half, placing the shortest sides together.

2. Unfold the card and cut across the fold.

3. Lay the two card pieces side by side.

4. Place the string across the cards so that there is about ½ inch (1.25 cm) between the cards. Tape the string to the cards.

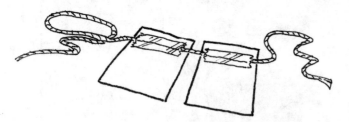

5. Bend the short end of each card over the string.

6. Tie the string around your head so that the short ends of the cards are against your forehead above each eye. If necessary, bend the cards so that the long end of each card sticks out over your eyes.

7. Wearing the sun visors will remind you of the camels waiting for Rebekah to bring them water. When friends ask about your sun visors, you can share the story of how God used camels to pick a bride for Isaac. *CAUTION: When you wear the sun visors outdoors, never look directly at the sun because doing so can permanently damage your eyes.*

—— Memory Verse ——

My help comes from the Lord. He is the Maker of heaven and earth. (Psalm 121:2)

—— Think about This ——

God helped the servant pick a bride for Isaac, and He helps camels because He made them with natural sun visors. How has God helped you?

Rebekah gave more help than was asked of her. How do you respond when people ask you to help them?

 # Joseph's Colorful Coat

Joseph's brothers saw that their father loved him more than any of them. So they hated Joseph. They couldn't even speak one kind word to him.—Genesis 37:4

Topic: Joseph's jealous brothers
Bible Exploration: Genesis 37, 41–45

Jacob was the son of Rebekah and Isaac. God changed Jacob's name to **Israel**. His descendants are called the **children of Israel** or **Israelites**, as well as **Hebrews** and **Jews**.

Israel had 12 sons, but he loved one of his sons more than the others. Israel's favorite son was Joseph. To show his special love for this son, Israel made Joseph a coat of different colors. Joseph's brothers were jealous of Joseph and his beautiful coat. To make things worse, Joseph had a dream that he was going to rule over his brothers. He was excited about the dream and told his brothers about it. The brothers were so angry at Joseph for having this

dream that they wanted to kill him. In the end, they didn't kill him, but they sold him as a slave, and he was taken to Egypt. To cover up their action, Joseph's brothers killed a lamb and spilled its blood on Joseph's coat. The bloody coat was given to their father so that he would think Joseph had been killed by a wild animal.

Joseph was a servant and a prisoner in Egypt, but the Lord stayed with him and gave him the wisdom to interpret the dreams of others. This skill became very useful when the **pharoah** (a term for an Egyptian king) had dreams that only Joseph was able to interpret. Eventually the pharoah gave Joseph the job of being his most important helper—the person in charge of storing food for the coming **famine** (a time when food is seriously scarce) that Joseph had seen in the pharaoh's dreams. In giving him this job, the pharaoh explained that Joseph was now a ruler over all of Egypt.

In time Joseph's brothers came to him for food, but they did not recognize him. When Joseph told them who he was, his brothers were afraid Joseph was going to punish them. But instead of being angry and punishing them, Joseph loved them and took care of them. This is because Joseph had **forgiven** his brothers, which means he had stopped being angry about what they had done to him.

In the following activity, you will make a beautiful and colorful paper coat to remind you to be forgiving like Joseph was. You can use as many different colors as you wish.

⎯ COLORFUL COAT ⎯

You Need scissors
six 4-by-6-inch (10-by-15-cm) pieces of construction paper (six different colors)
stick glue
sheet of 8½-by-11-inch (21.3-by-27.5-cm) white poster board

1. Cut pieces of different shapes and sizes from the colored construction paper.

2. Glue the colored pieces on the sheet of poster board. Leave some of the poster board uncovered so the white shows.

3. Allow the glue to dry, then fold the poster board sheet in half by placing the short sides together with the colored pieces inside.

4. Draw half of a coat on the folded paper as shown.

5. Cut out the coat, cutting through both layers of paper.

6. Open the paper coat.

7. Display the multicolored coat in your room to remind you that jealousy caused Joseph's brothers to try to harm him. But because Joseph was in the habit of asking God to direct him, he was able to forgive his brothers and help them.

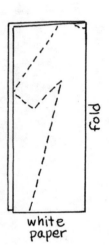

fold

white paper

⎯ Memory Verse ⎯

Forgive people when they sin against you. If you do, your Father who is in heaven will also forgive you. (Matthew 6:14)

⎯ Think about This ⎯

Joseph's brothers treated him very badly, but Joseph forgave them. If someone treats you badly, what will you do?

Moses's Basket

After that, she couldn't hide him any longer. So she got a basket that was made out of the stems of tall grass. She coated it with tar. Then she placed the child in it. She put the basket in the tall grass that grew along the bank of the Nile River. —Exodus 2:3

Topic: Moses's mother saves his life
Bible Exploration: Exodus 1–2:10

The book of Exodus begins with a story about a terrible command from the pharoah (the Egyptian king) that all male babies born to Hebrew (Israelite) women must be killed. The king wanted to control the number of male Hebrews in the land to prevent them from forming a strong army against the Egyptians.

Jochebed was the Hebrew mother of a baby boy. She did not want her baby killed, so she hid him for three months. When Jochebed could no longer hide her baby, she selected a basket that the young child would fit in. She made the basket **waterproof** (not letting water pass through) by covering it with tar. She put the

baby in the basket and set the basket in the Nile River near plants growing along the riverbank. Jochebed knew that the daughter of the pharoah bathed there. She did not know what the princess would do if she found the baby, but Jochebed trusted God to save her baby. She sent her older daughter, Miriam, to see what God was going to do with the baby.

When the princess came for her bath, she saw the basket and sent her maid to get it. When she opened the basket, she found a baby inside. The princess knew it was a Hebrew child, but she did not want the baby to be killed. Miriam came forward and offered to find a Hebrew woman to take care of the baby for the princess. The princess agreed and said she would pay the woman who took care of the baby. Miriam quickly returned to her mother and told her what had happened. Because of Miriam's quick thinking, Jochebed was hired to take care of her own baby. When the child was older, he was brought to the princess, and he became her son. The princess called the child Moses, which means drawn from the water. In time, Moses returned to his people and became their leader.

In the following activity, you will make a basket. Use as many different colors of craft sticks as you like. Strips of colored paper or ribbon can also be woven in through the craft sticks.

—BASKET—

You Need   3 sheets of newspaper
43 colored craft sticks, 4.52 by ⅜ by ¹⁄₁₂ inch (11.25 by 0.94 by 1.25 cm) each
liquid school glue

1. Lay the newspaper on a table to protect the table from glue.

2. Place 11 craft sticks side by side on the newspaper. These sticks will form the bottom of the basket.

3. Cover one side of a craft stick (stick 1) with glue, then place it across one side of the bottom of the basket as shown. Repeat with a second craft stick (stick 2) and place it on the other side.

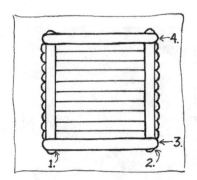

5. Repeat step 4, alternating the direction of the sticks until they are all used.

6. Your craft stick basket can be used to hold some of the things you care for. It will be a reminder of Moses's basket that held something that Jochebed greatly cared for—her son, Moses.

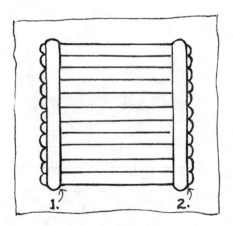

4. Cover the ends of sticks 1 and 2 with glue and place sticks 3 and 4 over the glue as shown.

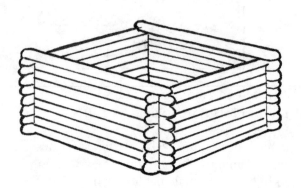

— Memory Verse —

Lord, hear me. Show me Your favor. Lord, help me. (Psalm 30:10)

— Think about This —

Jochebed had a very difficult problem, but God sent a princess to help her.
Do you have a problem that seems too difficult to solve?
Have you asked God for help?

8 Moses and the Burning Bush

There the angel of the Lord appeared to him from inside a burning bush. Moses saw that the bush was on fire. But it didn't burn up.—Exodus 3:2

Topic: God calls Moses

Bible Exploration: Exodus 3 and 4; Hebrews 11:24–27

Moses was a Hebrew (Israelite) who had been adopted by an Egyptian princess, but he remained faithful to his own people. In time he refused to be called the son of the princess. When he was 40 years old, he saw an Egyptian beating a Hebrew slave. He looked around and didn't see anyone watching, so he killed the Egyptian and buried him in the sand. But the Hebrew slave saw what Moses had done, and soon the pharoah knew too.

The pharoah (the Egyptian king), who also knew the truth about Moses's birth, thought Moses might try to lead the Hebrew slaves against the Egyptians, so he tried to kill Moses. But Moses ran away to another country, where he became a shepherd. Moses married and lived in his new land for 40 years.

After a while, the pharoah, the adopted grandfather of Moses, died. The Hebrew slaves prayed that God would help them, and He did. God had chosen Moses as the person to lead the Hebrews out of slavery before he was even born. Being adopted by the Egyptian princess was part of God's plan for Moses's life. Now God would reveal to Moses His plan for freeing the Hebrews.

One day while shepherding his flock of sheep, Moses saw a bush in flames. Amazed that the bush did not burn up, Moses got closer to it to see what was happening. He heard a voice coming from inside the bush calling his name. Moses answered, "Here am I." It was the voice of God. He told Moses not to come any closer and that he was to take off his shoes because the ground was **holy**, which meant that it was a very special place because God was present. God spoke to Moses and gave him directions so that Moses could lead God's people, the Hebrew slaves, to freedom.

In the following activity, you will make a paper bush to represent the one that Moses saw.

─── BURNING BUSH ───

You Need   three sheets of construction paper
                (2 green and 1 yellow)
                transparent tape
                red and orange crayons
                scissors

1. Lay the three sheets of paper end to end with their ends slightly overlapping and the yellow sheet on one end.

2. Tape the overlapping ends of the paper together.

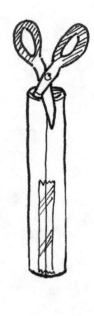

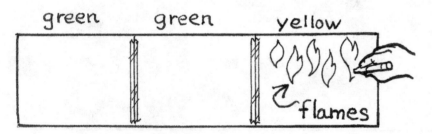

3. Use the crayons to draw flames on both sides of the yellow paper.

4. Starting at the yellow paper end, roll the combined paper sheets into a tube. To prevent the tube from unrolling, tape about one-half of the free overlapping edge.

5. Insert the scissors into the top of the tube and make four vertical cuts equally spaced around the tube. Cut through all the layers and make each cut go about halfway down the tube. Make the first cut along the overlapping edge that is not taped.

6. Bend down the cut pieces as shown.

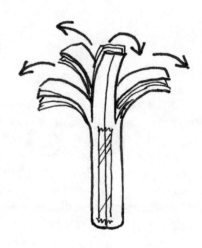

7. Hold the bottom of the roll with one hand and with the other pull the inside pieces upward. The bush grows as you continue to pull the pieces farther out. You will see the fire in the center of the bush.

8. You can stand the burning bush in your room to remind you that God loved Moses and had a good plan for his life. God also loves you and has a good plan for your life.

⟞ Memory Verse ⟞

"I know the plans I have for you," announces the Lord.
"I want you to enjoy success. I do not plan to harm you.
I will give you hope for the years to come." (Jeremiah 29:11)

⟞ Think about This ⟞

Are you worried about something that might happen? Share your worries
with a parent or a special friend. Together you can ask God
to help you follow His plan to solve your problems.

9 The Ten Commandments

The tablets were the work of God. The words had been written by God. They had been carved on the tablets.—Exodus 32:16

Topic: God's rules are given to Moses
Bible Exploration: Exodus 4:11–17, 7–11, 20:1–26, 32:1–16

God made Moses the leader of the Israelites. But first the pharaoh (the Egyptian king) had to release the people so that they could travel to the land God had promised for them. Moses didn't think he was good at speaking with people, so God sent Aaron, Moses's brother, to speak for Moses. Because it was God's plan,

despite the attempts of Moses and Aaron, the pharaoh refused to release the Israelites.

God sent **plagues** (things that cause widespread trouble and even death) on the Egyptians to convince the pharaoh to free the Israelites. There were plagues of frogs, lice, flies, death of livestock, boils, hail, locusts, and darkness. The plagues only affected the Egyptians, not the Israelites. Finally, when the firstborn son in each Egyptian family died, the pharaoh agreed to release the Israelites.

Again, according to God's plan, as soon as the Israelites left, the pharaoh changed his mind and sent an army to stop them. The Egyptian army chased the Israelites and thought they were trapped when they reached the Red Sea. The water was too deep to walk through. But God told Moses to hold his wooden staff and to stretch his hand out over the water. When Moses reached his hand out, the Lord sent a strong wind that not only pushed the waters back but dried the land. Moses led the Israelites across the sea on dry land.

When all the Israelites were safely on the other side of the sea, the Egyptian army attempted to cross along the same path. The Lord told Moses to reach out his hand again over the water, and when he did, the walls of water covered the entire Egyptian army.

The Israelites were finally free to travel to the land promised to them by God. When they reached Mount Sinai, God called Moses to come up on the mountain. It was here that God gave Moses laws about what is right and wrong. God wrote them on two stone tablets. Part of these laws are called the Ten Commandments. The Ten Commandments are: (1) Do not put any other gods in place of Me. (2) Do not make statues of gods that look like anything in the sky or on the earth or in the waters. Do not bow down to them or worship them. (3) Do not misuse the name of the Lord your God. (4) Remember to keep the Sabbath day holy. (5) Honor your father and mother. (6) Do not commit murder. (7) Do not commit adultery. (8) Do not steal. (9) Do not give false witness against your neighbor. (10) Do not long for anything that belongs to your neighbor.

The two stone tablets with all the rules, including the Ten Commandments, were kept in a special chest. This large gold chest was called the **ark of the covenant**. God gave Moses instructions on how the ark was to be built and told him that only **priests** of God (men in charge of worship activities and holy things of the true God) were allowed to carry or touch it.

In time the Israelites reached Canaan, the promised land. None of the people who had crossed the Red Sea, including Moses, crossed the Jordan River into Canaan. Only the new generation entered the land. Their new leader, chosen by God, was Joshua.

In the following activity, you will make a book containing the Ten Commandments.

—— TEN COMMANDMENTS ——

You Need   ruler
pencil
3 sheets of white copy paper
transparent tape
marker
pen

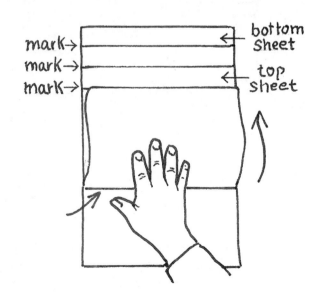

1. Use the ruler and the pencil to make a 1-inch (2.5-cm) mark from the top of each sheet of paper on the left side.

2. Place the three sheets of paper together with the edge of each sheet aligned with the mark on the paper below it.

3. Bring the bottom edge of the top sheet up and align its edge with the mark at its top. Press down on the folded edge of the paper.

4. Use tape to secure the folded edge to the paper below it.

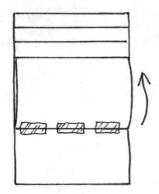

5. Fold over the next paper. Press down and tape as shown.

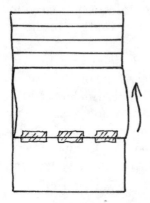

6. Fold over the bottom paper as shown. Press down on the fold. You have made a layered book.

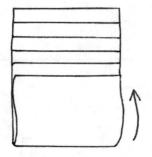

7. Turn the layered book as shown.

8. Use the marker to draw a semicircle at the top of the book as shown.

9. Using the pen, write "The Ten Commandments" on the first layer of the book within the arc. Then print numbers 1 through 10 on the other layers of the book as shown.

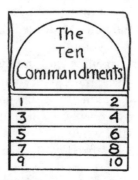

10. Raise the first layer with the title printed on it. Use the pen to write the first commandment on the left side of the next sheet and the second commandment on the right side of the next sheet. Continue lifting the pages and writing the commandments.

11. Read your layered book periodically to remind you of God's laws.

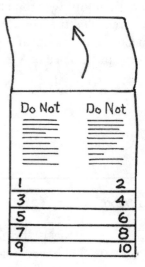

Memory Verse

Love the Lord your God. Do what He requires. Always obey His rules, laws, and commands. (Deuteronomy 11:1)

Think about This

Rules help you know how to behave so that you are safe and can get along with others. What are some of the rules at your home? At school? How does obeying God's rules help you to obey rules at home or at school?

Joshua: The New Leader

The priest will carry the ark of the Lord. He's the Lord of the whole earth. As soon as the priests step into the Jordan, it will stop flowing. The water that's coming down the river will pile up in one place. That's how you will know that the living God is among you.—Joshua 3:13

Topic: Joshua leads the Israelites across the Jordan River

Bible Exploration: Joshua 1, 3, and 4

After Moses died, God made Joshua the leader of the Israelites. His first job was to take all of the Israelites across the Jordan River into the Promised Land called Canaan. This was no small task because the river was very deep and even the banks were flooded with water. There was no bridge to walk across or boats to carry the people across the water. It had been 40 years since Moses led the Israelites out of Egypt. None of these Israelites had been in Egypt, so they had not seen the parting of the Red Sea. Joshua was not worried because God had told him that He would be with him. God told Joshua exactly what to do.

Joshua sent a messenger telling the people and the priests to get ready to cross the river. When the people saw the priests carrying the ark of the covenant toward the river, they were to follow. But they were not to get any closer than 3,000 feet (900 m) from the holy chest so that all could see it and be guided by it. As soon as the priests' feet touched the water, the river stopped flowing and the waters moved far upstream. The priests stood on dry land in the middle of the river while the people crossed.

Joshua picked one man from each of the 12 tribes and told them to pick up a stone from the riverbed where the priests were standing. The stones were used to make a memorial at Gilgal, a city near the river. The stones are a reminder that God caused the waters of the Jordan to stop flowing so that the Israelites could cross on dry ground.

After the people had crossed, the priests walked to the other side of the Jordan. Then the river water returned to its natural place.

In the following activity, a paperweight will be made from 12 stones.

— STONE PAPERWEIGHT —

You Need   large plastic bowl
tap water
12 small stones (collected from out-
    doors or aquarium stones)
toothbrush (one that will not be used
    to brush teeth)
paper towels
acrylic paints, 4 or more colors
paintbrush
liquid school glue

1. Fill the bowl about half full with water.

2. Put the stones in the bowl of water.

3. Using the toothbrush, clean each stone and dry it with a paper towel.

4. Paint each stone a different color and/or add designs such as dots. The paints can be mixed to produce different colors.

5. Allow the paint to dry. Then stack the stones together, using the glue to secure them in position.

6. When the glue has dried, the stones can be used as a paperweight. It will remind you that God was powerful enough to separate the waters of the Jordan River so that the Israelites could cross on dry land, and He is just as powerful and awesome today!

— Memory Verse —

He turned the Red Sea into dry land. The people of Israel passed through the waters on foot. Come, let us be full of joy because of what He did. (Psalm 66:6)

— Think about This —

Parting the waters of the Jordan River was awesome.
Can you think of other examples of God's awesome power?

The Walls of Jericho

The priests blew the trumpets. As soon as the fighting men heard the sound, they gave a loud shout. Then the wall fell down. Every man charged straight in. So they took the city.—Joshua 6:20

Topic: Joshua and the battle of Jericho
Bible Exploration: Joshua 6:1–27

Joshua led the Israelites across the Jordan River into the land of Canaan, their promised land, but there were people already living there. In order to live in Canaan, the Israelites would have to fight for possession of their land. With God on their side, they knew they would win.

Jericho was the first city the Israelites had to conquer. This city was protected by a tall, thick wall. The Lord sent a messenger telling Joshua how to conquer the city without fighting.

Joshua and the Israelites were to march around the city once every day for six days. The soldiers were to lead the march, followed by the priests with the ark of the covenant held on their shoulders, and finally the rest of the Israelites. During this march only the priests were to make any sound, and they loudly blew their trumpets. This was done every day for six days.

On the seventh day, they marched around the city seven times. The first six times were the same as before. The seventh time, the priests blew their trumpets as before, but Joshua said to the people, "Shout! For the Lord has given you the city." When the people shouted, the walls crashed to the ground. The walls didn't fall because of the loud sound. Instead, God caused the walls to fall and the city to be conquered without a fight because the Israelites had obeyed Him. Later the city of Jericho was rebuilt in a new place.

In the following activity, you will make a megaphone. It will remind you that great and wonderful things can happen if you obey God, just as they did for the Israelites.

— MEGAPHONE —

You Need   pencil
    22-by-28-inch (55-by-70-cm) piece of poster board
    yardstick (meterstick)
    drawing compass
    26-inch (65-cm) piece of string
    scissors
    crayons and/or markers
    transparent tape

1. Use the pencil to mark a dot in the center of one of the longer sides of the poster board, 14 inches (16.5 cm) from the corners.

2. Place the point of the compass on the dot and draw a semicircle with a diameter of 2 inches (5 cm).

3. Tie a loop in one end of the string.

4. Insert the pencil point through the loop, then place the point at one corner of the marked side of the poster board. Pull the string over the dot and hold the string on this dot with your finger. Using the pencil and the string as a drawing compass, draw a semicircle (half circle) by moving the pencil across the poster board to the other corner of the marked side.

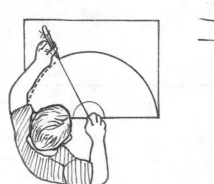

5. Cut out the small circle, then cut out the larger circle. Keep the curved piece and discard the remaining piece of poster board.

6. Use the markers and/or crayons to decorate the cutout. Stickers can also be used for decoration.

7. Shape the cutout into a cone by overlapping and taping the straight sides so that the decorated part is on the outside. You have made a megaphone with a small opening to cheer through.

8. You can use your megaphone to cheer loudly for your team at a sports event. Your friends may want to make one, so share the instructions as well as the story of how the walls of Jericho came down.

— Memory Verse —

Shout to the Lord with joy, everyone on earth.
Burst into joyful songs and make music. (Psalm 98:4)

— Think about This —

Are you part of a church choir? If you don't like to sing, what are other ways that you shout to the Lord with joy?

12 Achan's Treasure

Achan replied, "It is true! I've sinned against the Lord, the God of Israel. Here is what I've done. I saw a beautiful robe from Babylonia among the things we had taken. I saw five pounds of silver. And I saw a gold bar that weighed twenty ounces. I wanted them, so I took them. I hid them in the ground inside my tent. The silver is on the bottom."—Joshua 7:20–21

Topic: Disobedience causes others to suffer
Bible Exploration: Joshua 6:24, 7:1–26

Before the city of Jericho was destroyed, God had made a covenant with the Israelites. God told the people that everything in Jericho was to be destroyed except for things made of silver, gold, bronze, and iron, which were to be given to the priests because these treasures belonged to the Lord. If the Israelites kept the covenant, God would protect them in the battles necessary for them to take possession of their land.

After the walls of Jericho fell and the city was conquered, the Israelites felt sure God would keep His promise and they would easily win their next battle. Since their enemy had only a few fighting men, the Israelites sent a small group to defeat them. Instead of the easy victory they expected, they were badly beaten. The reason wasn't sending too few fighters; instead it was because of the disobedience of one man, Achan.

Achan had not obeyed God and had kept some of the treasure he found in Jericho for himself.

He dug a hole in the ground inside his tent and hid the treasure. While the treasure was hidden from the sight of other people, it was not hidden from God. Because of one man's disobedience, many people suffered. Achan had sinned against God. When Achan had been punished for his sin, God again protected the Israelites.

In the following activity, a penny is placed inside an envelope where it cannot be seen. The coin represents the hidden treasure that Achan stole. The coin is thicker than the paper, so when a crayon is rubbed across the paper above the coin, more of the crayon rubs off in this spot. This causes the shape of the coin to be darker and more visible. An impression of the coin is formed and revealed.

——HIDDEN TREASURE——

You Need   penny
             white envelope
             pencil
             crayon

1. Place the penny inside the envelope.

2. Use the pencil to write "Achan's Hidden Treasure" on the envelope.

3. Color the envelope with the crayon. An impression of the coin will form.

4. Turn the envelope over so that the coin impression is not visible. Then ask a friend to color the opposite side of the envelope. While he or she is coloring, you can share the story about Achan and how he tried to hide stolen treasure from God. Achan's disobedience affected not only his life but the lives of others. This is true for everyone. Lying or stealing affects your friends and family, so you shouldn't do it.

—— Memory Verse ——

"If you love Me, you will obey what I command." (John 14:15)

—— Think about This ——

God commands us to be honest and not to steal. Achan stole treasure and lied about it. Is Achan's sin any different from cheating on a test or saying you didn't do something when you really did?

13 David: The Giant Killer

"The Lord saved me from the paw of the lion. He saved me from the paw of the bear. And He'll save me from the powerful hand of this Philistine too." Saul said to David, "Go. And may the Lord be with you."—1 Samuel 17:37

Topic: David and Goliath
Bible Explorations: 1 Samuel 17

David was the youngest of Jesse's eight sons. David took care of his father's sheep in the pasture fields and stayed with them day and night. Sometimes wild animals tried to kill the sheep, but David protected them by throwing rocks with a **sling** (a piece of leather used to throw small objects). Often at night, David played his harp and sang songs about God's love and protection. He knew that God protected him even more than he did his sheep.

King Saul was the leader of the Israelites. There was a war between the Israelites and the Philistines. David's three oldest brothers were in the Israelite army. A Philistine giant named Goliath challenged the Israelites. Goliath told them to choose one man to fight him. The army of the man who lost would be the servants of the winning army. Goliath shouted his challenge every morning and evening for 40 days. This giant struck fear in the hearts of all the men in King Saul's army.

One day Jesse sent David to take food to his brothers in the army. When David arrived at the camp, he heard Goliath yelling across the valley. The Israelite soldiers were frightened, but David wasn't. He knew that God would help him, so he went to King Saul and volunteered to fight the giant. King Saul said no at first because David was young and not a trained soldier. But David explained how skillful he was in protecting his father's sheep with his sling. If he could fight off wild animals, he was sure God would help him fight Goliath. So the king agreed to let David fight the giant. David carried only his sling and five smooth stones in his shepherd's bag. In the end, David would need only one stone. With God's help, he slung the stone toward the giant, and it hit the giant's forehead and killed him. Once again God had come to the rescue of His people, caring for them like a shepherd caring for his beloved sheep.

In the following activity, a sack of rice is thrown so that it hits a mark. When testing your throwing skills, think of how difficult it was for David to hit the mark on the giant's head.

—— ON THE MARK ——

You Need   1 cup (250 ml) uncooked rice
white crew sock
circle of corrugated cardboard with a
    6-inch (15-cm) diameter
pencil

1.   Pour the rice into the sock. Tie a knot in the sock as close to the rice as possible. The sock has a ball of rice on one side of the knot and a loose end, which will be the handle, on the other side.

2.   Lay the cardboard circle on the ground in an open area outdoors.

3.   Stand with your toes against one side of the circle, then take 10 giant steps backward. Place the pencil at the end of your toes. The pencil will be the throwing line.

4.   Standing behind the pencil, hold the handle of the sock and toss the sock toward the circle. The goal is to have all of the rice ball part of the sock on the circle target. The handle doesn't have to be on the circle.

5.   Invite friends to a contest of hitting the mark with the ball of rice. Let each person have five tosses. You can tell your friends that David chose five stones, but he needed only one to kill the giant. See how many tosses each of you needs to hit the target.

—— Memory Verse ——

The Lord watches over you. The Lord is like a shade tree at your right hand. (Psalm 121:5)

—— Think about This ——

God helped David hit his mark and kill the giant. Do you have any "giant" problems? Have you asked for God's help?

14 Jonathan: David's Best Friend

Jonathan took off the robe he was wearing and gave it to David. He also gave him his military clothes. He even gave him his sword, his bow, and his belt.—1 Samuel 18:4

Topic: Jonathan saves his friend David
Bible Exploration: 1 Samuel 18–20

King Saul was the leader of the Israelites and Jonathan was his son. As the king's son, Jonathan would become the king when his father died. However, God had another plan that the king didn't know about. God had chosen a shepherd boy named David to be the next king of the Israelites.

The king was impressed that David was able to kill the Philistine giant Goliath, so he invited David to live in the palace. Jonathan and David became close friends. Because he loved David so much, Jonathan made a covenant with him that nothing would cause him to be a disloyal friend to David. Jonathan gave David his coat, uniform, sword, bow, and belt as symbols that he would protect David.

In time King Saul made David leader over the

soldiers. But as David continued to be successful in battles and the people loved him, King Saul became jealous and afraid of David. Finally King Saul told all his servants and Jonathan to kill David, but Jonathan protected David from his father. Even when King Saul told Jonathan that he would not become king as long as David was alive, Jonathan continued to protect his friend.

In the following activity, you will make friendship bracelets—one for you and one for each of your special friends. Jonathan gave David his coat as a sign of his friendship. You can give someone a bracelet as a sign of your friendship. The cardboard tube can be an empty toilet paper tube, or you can cut a piece from an empty paper towel tube.

—— FRIENDSHIP BRACELETS ——

You Need
scissors
empty cardboard tube
ruler
pencil
crayons and/or markers

1. Cut the cardboard tube down one side.

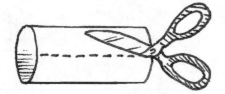

2. Use the ruler and the pencil to measure and mark sections about 1 inch (2.5 cm) wide on the tube. Cut the sections from the tube.

3. Use a marker to print "Friends" on the outside of the sections.

4. Use crayons and/or markers to decorate the sections. You have made friendship bracelets.

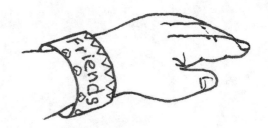

5. Give the bracelets to your special friends. You can tell them about Jonathan's special friendship with David. The bracelet wraps around your wrist just as God's love wraps around your heart. God loves you and is your very best friend.

—— Memory Verse ——

A friend loves at all times. He is there to help when trouble comes. (Proverbs 17:17)

—— Think about This ——

What makes a person a friend? Do you have friends like Jonathan?
Are you a friend like Jonathan was to David?

[15] Abigail's Generosity

Abigail didn't waste any time. She got 200 loaves of bread and two bottles of wine. The bottles were made out of animal skins. She got five sheep that were ready to be cooked. She got a bushel of grain that had been cooked. She got 100 raisin cakes. And she got 200 cakes of pressed figs. She loaded all of it on the backs of donkeys.—1 Samuel 25:18

Topic: Sharing
Bible Exploration: 1 Samuel 25:1–35

Abigail was the wife of Nabal, who was a very rich man. There are different kinds of riches. There are riches in what you have, such as silver and gold, and there are riches in what you do, such as sharing. There are also riches in

what you are, which is your character, such as being loving, kind, and generous. Nabal was only rich in what he had. He was mean and never shared his belongings. Abigail not only had many different kinds of riches but was very beautiful too.

The same David who killed Goliath heard that Nabal was shearing his sheep. It was customary to have a feast prepared during sheep-shearing season because it was a time of celebrating and sharing with others. David sent a message to Nabal that when his sheep and shepherds were out in the field and near where David and his men were, they helped the shepherds protect the sheep from being stolen or harmed. David sent men to Nabal requesting that food be prepared for them in exchange for this valuable service. Nabal should have honored David's request, but he refused. He didn't just say no but also insulted the men and David. The men returned and told David everything that Nabal had said. David told his men to prepare to attack. David planned to kill Nabal and everyone in his household.

One of the servants told Abigail about David's protecting Nabal's sheep as well as his shepherds. He also told her of how Nabal had insulted David's men. Abigail prepared food for David. Without telling her husband, she took it to David. She met David as he and his men were charging toward her home. She begged David not to take revenge on her husband and his household. David thanked Abigail for her food and advice because it had stopped him from his evil intentions. David knew that God sent Abigail to him, and he thanked God for this.

In the following activity, you will make a paper cup that you can use to share food or other things with friends or with the elderly in nursing homes.

—— FANCY HOLDER ——

You Need   sheet of white copy paper
scissors
crayons and/or markers

1. Fold one corner of the paper toward the opposite side to form a triangle.

2. Cut off the strip of paper that is left over and discard it.

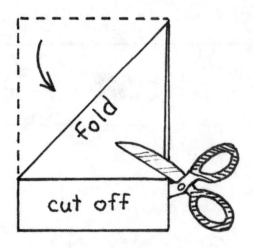

3. Turn the triangle so that the fold is at the bottom.

4. Fold corner A to touch point E, the center of the right side.

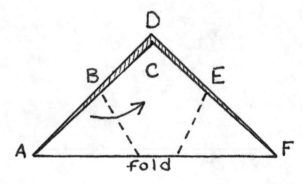

5. Fold corner F to touch point B, the center of the left side.

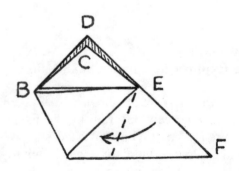

6. Fold corner C forward and corner D backward.

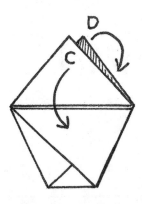

7. Pull the paper open to form a cup.

8. Use the crayons and/or markers to decorate the outside of the cup with colorful designs.

9. Use the cup to share something with someone who needs it. You may wish to make several cups so that you can share with more people.

— Memory Verse —

Do to others as you want them to do to you. (Luke 6:31)

— Think about This —

Are you treating everyone the way you want them to treat you?
If you are nice to people, is that a guarantee that they will be nice to you?
Why or why not?

16 Solomon: The Wisest Man

All of the people of Israel heard about the decision the king had given. That gave them great respect for him. They saw that God had given him wisdom. They knew that Solomon would do what was right and fair when he judged people.—1 Kings 3:28

Topic: King Solomon's wisdom
Bible Exploration: 1 Kings 3:5–13, 16–28

Wisdom is an understanding that comes from God. Being wise means to have the ability to make good decisions. Other than Jesus, King Solomon was the wisest person who ever lived on Earth. God appeared to King Solomon in a dream and told him he could have anything he wanted. Most people would ask for money or

things. But King Solomon asked God for wisdom so that he could be a good king. God was pleased with Solomon's request and gave him great wisdom. King Solomon used his wisdom to help people solve problems that they couldn't solve themselves.

There were once two women who claimed to be the mother of the same baby. Both of these women had given birth, but in the night one baby had died. The mother of the dead baby stole the living baby from his mother. The women went to King Solomon and asked him to decide who the baby really belonged to. King Solomon said he would split the baby in half and give one-half to each woman. One woman said not to kill the baby but to give him to the other woman. The other woman said if she couldn't have the baby, then no one could, so the baby should be divided. King Solomon knew who was the real mother of the child because he listened carefully to what the two women said. The wise king knew that the real mother would rather give her baby away than see him harmed.

Owls are a symbol of wisdom. In the following activity, you will make an owl puppet as a reminder of King Solomon's great wisdom.

⸺ A WISE BIRD ⸺

You Need   copy of Owl Parts (see the next page)
scissors
glue stick
brown paper lunch bag
black and brown crayons

1.   Make a photocopy of the Owl Parts page.

2.   Cut out the face, then cut across the dashed cutting line.

3.   Glue the larger upper part of the face on the flap of the bag, the part formed by the bottom of the bag. Glue the smaller lower part of the face on the bag below the flap so that the two pieces are in line with each other as shown.

bottom of bag

4.   Use the black crayon to color the beak and the feet. Use the brown crayon to color the wings.

5.   Cut out the beak, feet, and wings. Glue these parts to the bag as shown.

6.   Use the black crayon to draw curved lines on the bag to represent feathers.

7.   The puppet owl will be a reminder for you to ask God for wisdom.

⸺ Memory Verse ⸺

If any of you need wisdom, ask God for it. He will give it to you.
God gives freely to everyone. He doesn't find fault. (James 1:5)

⸺ Think about This ⸺

What problems do you have that you need more wisdom to solve?
Have you asked God for wisdom?

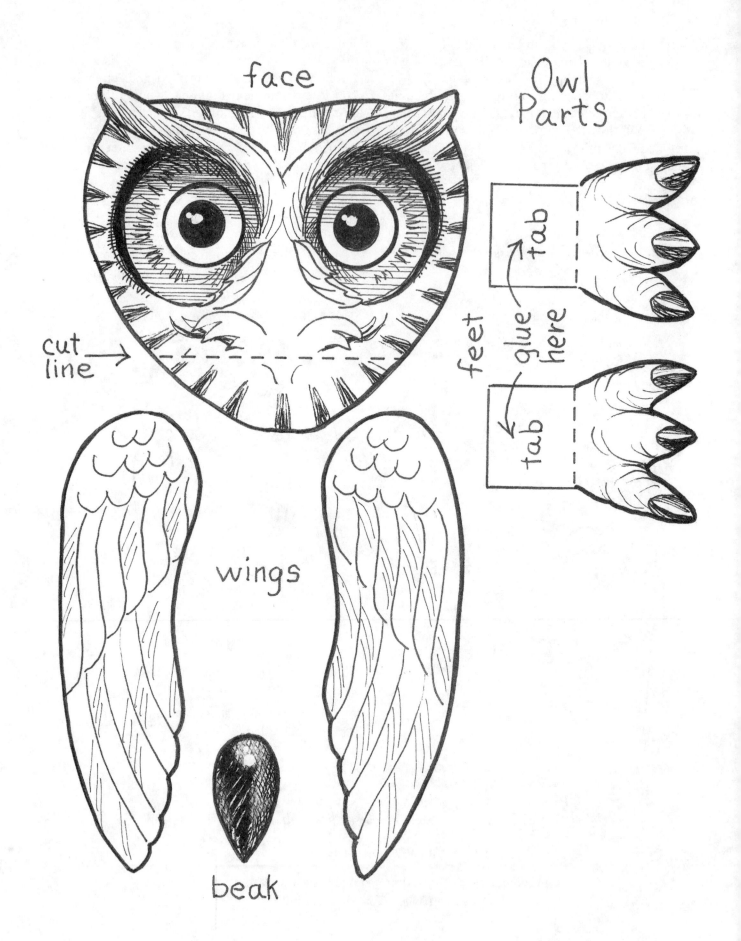

face

Owl Parts

cut line →

feet

tab

glue here

tab

wings

beak

17 Elijah: God's Messenger

All of the people saw it. Then they fell down flat with their faces toward the ground. They cried out, "The Lord is the one and only God! The Lord is the one and only God!"—1 Kings 18:39

Topic: Elijah proves that there is only one true God

Bible Exploration: 1 Kings 18:16–39

King Ahab was the most wicked king who ever ruled over Israel. He was married to Jezebel, who was also very wicked as well as being a **priestess** (a woman who directs worship activities) to a false god named Baal. Jezebel declared that Baal would be the official god of Israel. The Israelites were afraid of King Ahab and Jezebel, so many worshiped both God and Baal. Elijah was a **prophet** (a messenger from

God) of the true God. He worshiped only God, and God's message to the Israelites was that they must decide whom they were going to serve: either the Lord, the true God, or Baal, a false god. Elijah had King Ahab call all the prophets of Baal (messengers of Baal) to Mount Carmel for a contest. There were to be two altars built, one for God and one for Baal. The 450 prophets of Baal were to pray that Baal would cause the sacrifice upon his altar to catch on fire, and Elijah would pray to God to set His sacrifice on fire.

For hours the Baal prophets prayed, but no

fire came. Although Elijah even poured buckets of water over God's altar so that it was soaking wet, he trusted that his God would set the wet wooden altar on fire. When he started to pray, fire instantly came and burned up the altar, the sacrifice, the stones, and even the dirt around the altar. This was truly a miracle (an amazing thing that only God can do). The Israelites saw this great miracle of God, and they believed and trusted that God is the true god.

In the following activity, a trick demonstrates something that you have to see to believe: paper clips that are linked without being touched.

——— CONNECT THE CLIPS ———

You Need   2-by-8-inch (5-by-20-cm) strip of paper
2 metal paper clips

1. Fold one end of the paper strip so that the end touches the strip just past the middle.

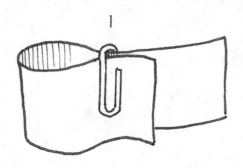

2. Secure the end of the strip with one of the paper clips as shown.

3. Fold the other end of the paper around the back side of the strip and secure it with the other paper clip, shown in clip 2.

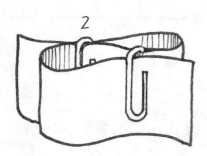

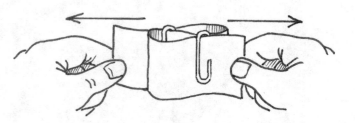

4. Holding the ends of the folded paper, slowly pull them in opposite directions until the paper is stretched out.

5. The paper straightens and the paper clips pop off attached to each other. *CAUTION: Make sure the combined paper clips do not pop toward your face or the faces of others.*

6. Practice a few times, then demonstrate the trick to friends. First explain that you have a trick that they will have to see to believe. Prepare the paper with the paper clips on it in advance. Before pulling the ends of the paper, say that you are going to cause the paper clips to link together. Once you have demonstrated the feat, share the secret of how the paper clips were attached to the paper. You can also share the story of Elijah and the fire, another event that had to be seen to be believed. Point out that while linking the paper clips was a trick, the fire was a miracle caused by God.

——— Memory Verse ———

But You are the only true God. You are the only living God. You are the King who rules forever. (Jeremiah 10:10a)

——— Think about This ———

What have you seen that makes you know that the Lord is God?

18 Queen Esther's Dinner Guests

*Esther replied, "King Xerxes, if it pleases you, come to a big dinner today.
I've prepared it for you. Please have Haman come with you."—Esther 5:4*

Topic: Esther risks her life to save her people
Bible Exploration: Esther 1–10

Esther was a young Jewish girl who married the king of Persia. The king loved Esther very much. The king had a prime minister named Haman. Because of Haman's hatred for the Jews (the Israelites), he tricked the king into agreeing to a law that would get rid of all the Jews in his kingdom. Neither Haman nor the king knew that Esther was Jewish. Mordecai, Esther's cousin who raised her after her parents died, had advised her to keep this a secret.

Mordecai got a message to Esther about the new law and begged her to go to the king. No one, including the queen, could appear before the king without being summoned. Doing so would mean that person could be put to death. But Mordecai said that God might have made Esther queen so that she would be in a position to save her people.

Esther made her appearance before the king, who was pleased to see her. He said he would give her whatever she wanted, even half of his kingdom. She didn't tell the king about Haman just yet. Instead she asked that the king and Haman come to dinner. After the dinner, the king again asked Esther what she wanted, and Esther again asked that Haman and the king come for dinner the following night. At the second dinner, Esther finally told the king about Haman's trickery and begged the king to save her people. The king had Haman killed.

During this time a law could not be changed, so a second law was written giving the Jews the right to defend themselves. The bravery of Esther saved the Jews.

In the following activity, you will make a crown and use glitter and glue to make sparkling places on the crown that represent jewels.

——ROYAL CROWN——

You Need
    sheet of white copy paper
    scissors
    transparent tape
    6-by-12-inch (15-by-30-cm) piece of
        yellow construction paper
    pencil
    liquid school glue
    glitter

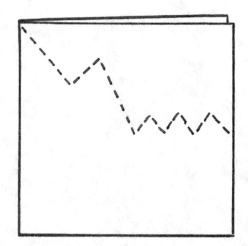

1. Fold the paper in half twice by placing the long sides together.

2. Unfold the paper and cut along the fold lines. You will have four strips of paper. Use three of the strips and discard the fourth one.

3. Tape the ends of the three paper strips together.

4. Wrap the paper band around your head across your forehead.

5. Holding the overlapping ends together, remove the paper band from your head.

6. Cut off any excess paper so that the ends of the paper band overlap about 2 inches (10 cm).

7. Fold the piece of construction paper in half with the short ends together.

8. Use the pencil to draw a design on the paper similar to the one shown.

9. Cut out the design through both layers of paper.

10. Lay the design in the middle of the paper band and tape it in place.

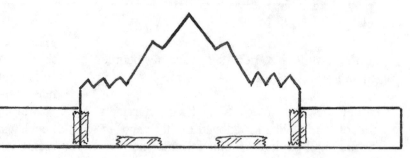

11. Add jewels to the crown by placing dots of glue on the design and covering the glue with glitter. Allow the glue to dry.

12. Wrap the paper band around your head and across your forehead so that the crown is in front. Then ask a helper to tape the ends of the band together. You have made a royal crown.

13. Wear your royal crown to remind you of the story of Queen Esther and how brave she was to appear before the king.

—— Memory Verse ——

A man may have many plans in his heart. But the Lord's purpose wins out in the end. (Proverbs 19:21)

—— Think about This ——

It was God's plan for Esther to become queen so that she could help her people. Who needs your help?

Jonah's Fish Tale

But the Lord sent a huge fish to swallow Jonah. And Jonah was inside the fish for three days and three nights.—Jonah 1:17

Topic: Jonah runs away from God
Bible Exploration: Jonah 1–2

Jonah was a prophet. God told Jonah to go to the city of Nineveh and tell the people that God would destroy them if they did not give up their evil ways and obey God. But Jonah didn't like the people in Nineveh, so he boarded a ship that was going in the opposite direction from Nineveh. God could have sent someone else to Nineveh, but He wanted Jonah to go, so God sent a great storm to stop him. The sailors on

the ship were afraid that it would sink. They prayed to their gods, but nothing happened.

Finally the sailors discovered that Jonah had disobeyed the Lord. Jonah suggested that they throw him into the sea because he knew the storm was his fault. The sailors didn't want to kill Jonah, so they tried harder to get back to land, but the storm grew worse. Finally they threw Jonah into the sea and the sea became calm.

God provided a big fish that swallowed Jonah. He stayed inside the fish for three days and nights. Jonah prayed a lot while he was in the belly of the fish. God answered his prayers and commanded the fish to spit Jonah onto dry land. God told Jonah a second time to go to Nineveh, and this time he immediately obeyed. As soon as the people of Nineveh heard Jonah's message, they stopped their evil acts and asked God to forgive them. God took pity on them and did not destroy them. When Jonah obeyed God, the lives of many people were changed.

In the following activity, you will make a three-dimensional fish to remind you that when you obey God, He can use you to do amazing things.

—— 3-D FISH ——

You Need   two 8½-by-11-inch (21.3-by-27.5-cm) sheets of white poster board
pencil
ruler
pen
scissors
crayons and/or markers
paper hole punch
12-inch (30-cm) piece of string

1. Fold one sheet of poster board in half by placing the long sides together.

2. Use the pencil to draw half of a fish on one side of the folded poster board.

3. Using the pencil and the ruler, start at the fold line and draw six lines 2 inches (5 cm) long and about 1 inch (2.5 cm) apart.

4. Use the pen to draw a stick figure to represent Jonah between the third and fourth lines.

5. Cut out the fish, cutting through both layers of the poster board.

6. With the poster board still folded, cut along the six lines through the fold and both layers of paper.

7. Unfold the fish.

8. Use crayons and/or markers to draw an eye, a mouth, and scales on the fish.

9. Cut a 2-by-10-inch (5-by-25-cm) strip from the second piece of poster board.

10. Starting on the back side of the fish, weave the poster board strip through the cuts in the fish's body. To make the fish three-dimensional, flip the strip so that it is perpendicular (90 degrees) to the fish. The ends of the strip should be on the back side of the fish. Jonah is on the front side.

11. Use the paper hole punch to make a hole in the top center edge of the fish.

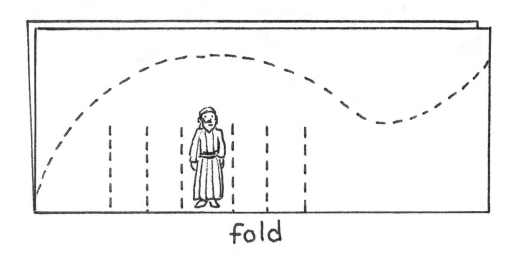

fold

12. Tie the string in the hole to form a loop.

13. Hang the fish in your room as a reminder that you should always obey God.

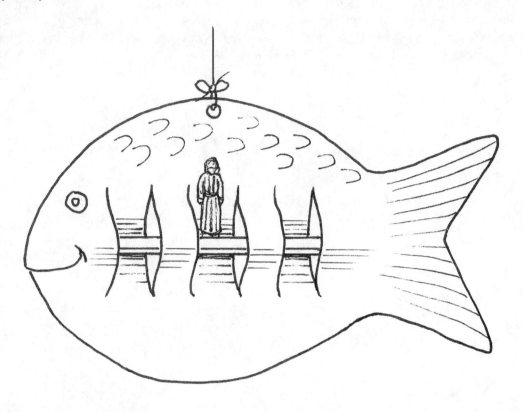

--- Memory Verse ---

Teach me to live as You command, because that makes me very happy. (Psalm 119:35)

--- Think about This ---

What were the results when Jonah did not obey God?
What happened when Jonah did obey God?
How can obeying God's commands make you happy?

THE NEW TESTAMENT

20 The Christmas Story

But the angel said to them, "Do not be afraid. I bring you good news of great joy. It is for all the people. Today in the town of David a Savior has been born to you. He is Christ the Lord."—Luke 2:10–11

Topic: Jesus Christ is born
Bible Exploration: Luke 1:26–35, 2:1–20; Matthew 2:1–12

About 2,000 years ago in the town of Nazareth, there lived a carpenter named Joseph and a young woman named Mary. Mary and Joseph were engaged. One day an angel, Gabriel, appeared to Mary and told her that God had chosen her to be the mother of His son. An angel also appeared in Joseph's dream and told him that he was to marry Mary and that Mary was to have a baby. The baby was God's son and they were to name him Jesus.

Soon after the angel's visit, Mary and Joseph married. When it was almost time for the baby to be born, they had to take a long trip to Bethlehem to pay a special tax. Mary had to ride on a donkey for several days. They were very tired when they reached Bethlehem and tried to find a room at an inn. Many people had come to pay the tax and all the inns were full. The only place available was in a stable with animals. That night Jesus, the Son of God, was born in the stable. Mary wrapped the baby in strips of cloth to keep him warm and laid him in a **manger** (a food box for animals) filled with hay.

That same night an angel appeared to shepherds who were in their fields watching over their sheep. At first the shepherds were frightened, but the angel told them not to be afraid. He had come to tell them the good news that a savior had been born in the town of David, which was Bethlehem. The angel identified the savior as **Christ** or **Messiah**, both meaning the Anointed One. The savior is also called **Immanuel**, meaning God is with us.

The shepherds left the field and went to Bethlehem. There they found Baby Jesus lying in a manger. After seeing the baby, the shepherds spread the news that Christ the Lord had been born. Far away in the east, wise men saw a new star in the sky. They knew that the star was a sign that the savior had been born. In time, the wise men arrived in Bethlehem to worship Christ Jesus. To **worship** is to freely give love, honor, and praise. The wise men chose to show their love by giving Jesus gifts of gold, frankincense, and myrrh.

In the following activity, toothpicks will move on their own to form the shape of a five-pointed star to represent the Christmas star. Water will enter the broken ends of the toothpicks, causing the wood to expand. This expansion makes the toothpicks move. It is important that the wax paper be as flat as possible so that it doesn't restrict the motion of the toothpicks.

⸺ CHRISTMAS STAR ⸺

You Need   5 round wooden toothpicks
12-inch (30-cm) square of wax paper
eyedropper
cup of tap water

1. Bend each toothpick into a V shape without breaking it apart.

2. Lay the wax paper on a table and smooth the paper so that it is as flat as possible.

3. Place the bent toothpicks on the sheet of wax paper in a starburst pattern as shown in the diagram. Put the bent parts as close together as possible in the center.

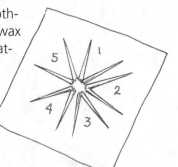

4. Fill the eyedropper with water from the cup.

5. Place 4 drops of water in the opening in the center of the starburst. You want the water to touch the bent part of each toothpick.

6. Watch and wait until all movement stops. A five-pointed star will form.

7. Share this activity with friends and tell them about the Christmas story and the Bethlehem star.

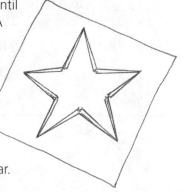

⸺ Memory Verse ⸺

Come, let us bow down and worship Him. Let us fall on our knees in front of the Lord our Maker. (Psalm 95:6)

⸺ Think about This ⸺

Worshiping is loving, honoring, and praising.
How do you worship the Lord?

21 Three in One

"So you must go and make disciples of all nations. Baptize them in the name of the Father and of the Son and of the Holy Spirit."—Matthew 28:19

Topic: The trinity
Bible Exploration: Isaiah 55:8–9; Matthew 3:16–17, 28:19; John 14:9–11, 14:6; 1 Corinthians 8:4; 1 Peter 1:2

The Bible clearly states that there is one God. But throughout the Bible, God is described as three **divine** (Godly) persons: God the Father, God the Son, and God the Holy Spirit. The word **trinity** is not found in the Bible, but it is a term that means the three divine persons of God united into one divine being called God.

While we can understand the definition of the trinity, it is impossible to understand what it really means. But it is no more impossible to understand the trinity than it is to understand **eternity**, which means time without end. We should not be surprised that with our human minds we don't understand everything about God. God even tells us in the Bible that our thoughts are not like His thoughts.

While the three divine persons of God are never separated from one another, the Bible does give a basic description for each. God the

Father is primarily viewed as the Creator and the Source of Life. God the Son is primarily viewed as the **Redeemer** because He is the one who **redeemed** (ransomed), which means to pay the price for the sins of others. God the Holy Spirit is primarily viewed as the Helper.

In the following activity, you will use one piece of clay to make pretzels, each with three equal-size openings. The pretzel represents the trinity, which is one God (a single piece of clay) in three divine persons (three equal-size openings).

——— CLAY PRETZELS ———

You Need   ½ (125 mL) cup flour
¼ (63 mL) cup table salt
bowl
½ (125 mL) cup warm tap water
12-inch (30-cm) piece of wax paper

1. Pour the flour and the salt into the bowl. Use your hands to thoroughly mix them together.

2. Pour about half of the water over the surface of the flour and salt mixture. With your hands, mix until it makes a smooth dough. If the mixture is too dry, slowly add more water. If the dough feels too sticky, sprinkle a little flour on it.

3. Knead the dough for 2 to 3 minutes. You have made salt clay.

4. Shape the clay into four even-size balls.

5. Lay the wax paper on a table and place one of the clay balls in the center of the paper.

6. Roll the clay back and forth with your hands, forming a roll about 12 inches (30 cm) long.

7. Shape the clay roll into a pretzel as shown. Try to make three equal-size openings in the clay pretzel.

8. Repeat steps 6 and 7 for each of the three remaining balls of clay.

9. Allow the clay pretzels to air-dry. This will take two or more days. To speed the drying, periodically turn the pretzels over.

10. You can display the clay pretzels in your room as a reminder that the one God includes God the Father, God the Son, and God the Holy Spirit. Share the extra clay pretzels and what they represent with friends.

—— Memory Verse ——

There is only one God. And there is only one go-between for God and human beings. He is the man Christ Jesus. (1 Timothy 2:5)

—— Think about This ——

Who is your Lord and Savior? Who helps you understand the Bible so that you can know more about God?

22 Stormy Seas

The disciples were amazed. They asked, "What kind of man is this?
Even the winds and the waves obey Him."—Matthew 8:27

Topic: Jesus calms the storm
Bible Exploration: Matthew 8:23–27;
Luke 3:23

Jesus was about 30 years old when He began His special work on Earth for God the Father, which lasted about three years. While on Earth, Jesus had many **followers**, which were people who believed that Jesus is the Messiah. Followers of Jesus then and now are called **disciples**.

During one of their journeys together, Jesus and His chosen 12 disciples set out in a boat to cross the Sea of Galilee. The waters were calm, and Jesus fell asleep in the boat. A sudden storm blew in while he was sleeping. The disci-

ples were fearful that the boat might tip over or fill with water and sink. Jesus woke up and spoke to the wind and the sea. At His command, the wind and the sea became perfectly calm. The disciples were amazed at this miracle.

You may have storms in your life, such as friends who move away, pets that die, and maybe even parents who divorce. But at times when things are stormy and you are afraid, like the disciples, you too can call on Jesus. This doesn't mean that the bad things will stop happening, but it does mean that Jesus will provide a way for you to be comforted.

In the following activity you will discover a secret power that will make a paper boat move.

When the boat is placed in the water, the water molecules on the surface of the water pull on the boat in all directions. Placing soap on one side of the boat stops the pull of the water molecules on that side, so there is an uneven pulling on the boat. When one side doesn't pull as much as the other, the motion is toward the stronger-pulling side. The soap is the secret ingredient that makes the boat move.

—— SOAP-PROPELLED BOAT ——

You Need
pencil
1-by-1-inch (2.5-by-2.5-cm) piece of poster board
scissors
dishwashing liquid
2 saucers
tap water
toothpick

1. Use the pencil to draw a triangle on the piece of poster board. Write an X on one side of the triangle as shown.

2. Cut out the triangle from the poster board. You have made a paper boat.

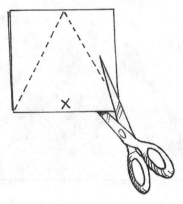

3. Pour a drop of dishwashing liquid in one of the saucers.

4. Pour just enough water into the other saucer to cover the bottom of the dish.

5. Set the paper boat on the surface of the water. Using the toothpick, move the boat so that the side with the X is near the edge of the saucer.

6. Dip the end of the toothpick into the drop of dishwashing liquid. Then touch the water near the X side of the boat with the wet end of the toothpick. The boat will move away from the soapy end.

7. Without Jesus in your life, you are like the paper boat that just floats on the water. But Jesus gives you the secret power that gets you through the storms in your life. Show the boat to your friends and explain its secret power. Tell them about your secret power—Jesus.

—— Memory Verse ——

God's power has given us everything we need to lead a godly life. All of that has come to us because we know the One who chose us. He chose us because of His own glory and goodness. (2 Peter 1:3)

—— Think about This ——

What problems do you have? Have you asked Jesus to help you overcome them? Remember that overcoming doesn't always mean the problem goes away; sometimes we are given power to live with our problems.

23 A Boy's Lunch

"Here is a boy with five small loaves of barley bread. He also has two small fish. But how far will that go in such a large crowd?" Then Jesus took the loaves and gave thanks. He handed out the bread to those who were seated. He gave them as much as they wanted. And He did the same with the fish.—John 6:9, 11

Topic: Jesus feeds the thousands
Bible Exploration: Matthew 14:13–20; John 6:1–15

Jesus and His disciples traveled to a quiet, peaceful place on the shores of Galilee so that they could rest. But a great multitude of people followed them. They came to hear Him teach and to be healed of sickness. Jesus was tired, but He lovingly talked to the people. Many were healed and comforted by Him.

In the evening Jesus said that the disciples should provide food for all the people. They didn't have enough money to buy food for the thousands of people, and the only food available was the lunch of a young boy in the crowd. The boy had brought two fish and five small loaves of bread to eat. This lunch was brought to Jesus. Jesus asked the people to sit down on the grass, then He gave thanks to God for the food. The disciples passed out the food, and there was enough for everyone. The people were amazed at this miracle performed by Jesus.

In the following activity, a small amount of colored soap will be used to make large amounts of colored bubbles. The bubbles will be collected to paint colorful pictures. This activity should be performed outdoors.

PAINT BUBBLES

You Need   yellow, red, and blue food coloring
dishwashing soap
three 5-ounce (150-mL) paper cups
3 drinking straws
2 sheets of 8½-by-11-inch (21.3-by-27.5-cm) white poster board

1. Pour 1 teaspoon (5 mL) of dishwashing liquid into each of the three paper cups.

2. Add 5 drops of yellow food coloring to one of the cups. Stir with one of the straws. Leave the straw standing in the cup of colored soap.

3. Repeat step 2 twice, adding red food coloring to the second cup and blue food coloring to the third cup. Use a clean straw for each cup.

4. Lay one of the sheets of poster board on an outdoor table.

5. Lift the straw in the yellow-colored soap.

6. Place the dry end of the straw in your mouth with the wet end near the piece of poster board. Blow through the straw. *CAUTION: Make sure you do not inhale when the straw is in your mouth.*

7. Repeat steps 5 and 6 until the poster board is covered with yellow bubbles. Then place the second piece of poster board on top of the bubbles and gently press it down until all the bubbles have popped. Remove the top sheet of poster board and lay it paint side up on the table.

8. Repeat steps 5 and 6 twice more. First use the straw in the blue-colored soap, then use the straw in the red-colored soap.

9. Both sheets of poster board will have colorful designs. Allow the sheets to dry.

10. You have made two pieces of art. Display one in your room to remind you of the fish and loaves miracle, and share the other with a friend. You can also repeat steps 2 and 3 for your friend, and tell him or her that the number and size of the bubbles as compared to the size of the soap drop reminds you of a Bible story. Tell your friend about the miracle of the loaves and the fishes.

— Memory Verse —

Give thanks no matter what happens. God wants you to thank Him because you believe in Christ Jesus. (1 Thessalonians 5:18)

— Think about This —

It is easy to be thankful for good things, such as food that you like. But it is hard to be thankful for food that you don't like even though you know it is good for you. What things are you thankful for even though you don't really like them? Medicine? School?

[24] The One to Turn To

Right away Jesus reached out His hand and caught him. "Your faith is so small!" He said. "Why did you doubt Me?"—Matthew 14:31

Topic: Peter walks on water
Bible Exploration: Matthew 14:22–36

After using a boy's lunch of two fish and five loaves of bread to feed thousands of people, Jesus told His disciples to get into their boat and cross to the other side of the Sea of Galilee. When they left, Jesus sent the people away and went to a mountain where He could be alone to pray. It was nighttime when He finished praying and started walking across the water toward the boat.

A storm caused huge waves to toss the boat around. When the disciples saw Jesus walking across the water, they were afraid that He was a ghost. Jesus told them not to be afraid. Peter, who was adventurous and bold, asked Jesus if he could come to Him. Jesus said yes. When Peter got out of the boat, he trusted that Jesus would give him the power to walk on the water, and Jesus did. But when Peter took his eyes off of Jesus, he realized the danger he was in. His fear made him doubt that he could walk on water, and he began to sink. At that moment, Peter's faith was small.

Peter had been a fisherman, so he could swim. But he did not try to save himself; instead he cried out to Jesus. In a time of great trouble, Peter turned to Jesus for help. Jesus immediately stretched out His hand and picked Peter up. When they got into the boat, the storm stopped. Peter's walking on the water was a miracle. Even though Peter's faith was small, the important thing is that his faith was in Jesus.

In the following activity, you will make a paper figure of Peter that will stand on water. It was a miracle that Peter could stand on water, but your version doesn't sink because surface tension makes the water act as if it has a thin skin on it.

━ WATER WALKER ━

You Need   4-by-6-inch (10-by-15-cm) unlined index card
pencil
scissors
colored markers
large bowl
tap water

1. Fold the index card in half with the long sides together.

2. Use the pencil and the pattern shown to draw a figure of Peter on the card.

3. Cut out the figure, cutting through both layers of the card.

4. Bend the 2-inch (5-cm) section below the figure's feet so that it is perpendicular (at a 90-degree angle) to the figure. This section forms a stand for the figure.

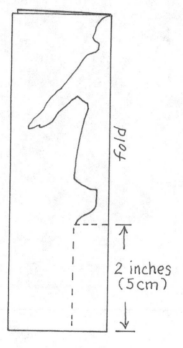

fold

2 inches (5cm)

5. Use the markers to draw and color in facial features and clothes on the figure.

6. Fill the bowl about three-quarters full with water.

7. Gently stand Peter on the surface of the water in the bowl.

8. Share this activity with a friend, and make other figures of Peter that stand on water. You can share the story of how Peter walked on water.

━ Memory Verse ━

But when you ask, you must believe. You must not doubt. People who doubt are like waves of the sea. The wind blows and tosses them around. (James 1:6)

━ Think about This ━

Why could Peter walk on water? Why did he sink? Whom did Peter turn to when he was in trouble? Whom can you turn to when you are in trouble?

Jesus Heals

Jesus reached out His hand and touched the man. "I am willing to do it,"
He said. "Be 'clean'!" Right away the disease left him.—Luke 5:13

Topic: Jesus cures a leper
Bible Exploration: Luke 5:12–16

Long ago when Jesus was living on Earth, **leprosy** was one of the most dreaded diseases. There was no cure for it, and it was thought to be God's punishment for sin. Leprosy is a disease that causes sores on the body. It also causes a loss of feeling or numbness in the hands, feet, legs, and arms. Leprosy was very contagious. People with leprosy had to leave their family and friends and never go near them again. There was even a law that they had to warn others of their presence by shouting, "Unclean! Unclean!"

If having leprosy was a punishment by God,

then Jesus would not have wanted to heal a leper. In one of the cities that Jesus visited, a leper who believed that Jesus was the Son of God decided to find out if his disease was God's will. The man disobeyed the law requiring him to stay away from people and asked Jesus to heal him. The man approached Jesus and kneeled before Him. Instead of shouting, "Unclean!" he said, "Lord, if You are willing to make me 'clean,' You can do it."

No one at that time would touch a leper, but Jesus reached out His hand and touched the man, saying, "I am willing to do it." Immediately the disease left the man's body. This healing proved that leprosy was a disease just like all diseases and not a punishment from God. Today leprosy is still one of the major health problems in some undeveloped countries even though the disease can be cured.

In the following activity, the numbness that you will feel in your finger is not real, but it is a trick caused by the messages sent to your brain. The numbness represents the real feeling for a leper. When you rub both sides of your finger, messages are sent from the finger that is rubbed as well as from the fingers doing the rubbing. The combination of these messages tells your brain that both sides of your finger have feeling. But when you place a pencil on one side of your finger, the combined messages tell your brain that only one side of your finger has feeling.

⟶ TRICKED ⟶

You Need   pencil

1. With the thumb and index finger of one hand, rub both sides of the index finger of your other hand.

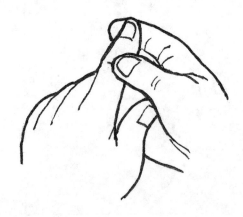

2. Place the pencil against the palm side of the index finger of one hand. Hold the pencil in place using the fingers and thumb of the same hand.

3. Repeat step 1, but rub the pencil with the index finger instead of the underside of the finger. Even though you know that you are rubbing the pencil instead of your finger, your brain is tricked into thinking that one side of your finger is numb.

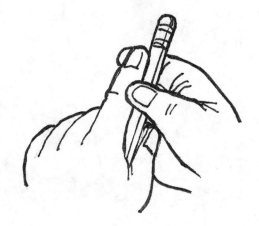

4. Show this trick to your friends and tell them the story of how Jesus healed the leper.

⟶ Memory Verse ⟶

You who have respect for the Lord, trust in Him. He helps you.
He is like a shield that keeps you safe. (Psalm 115:11)

⟶ Think about This ⟶

When you are sick, what are some of the ways the Lord helps you to get well? Medicine? A doctor? Your mom?

26 Too Busy!

"Martha, Martha," the Lord answered. "You are worried and upset about many things. But only one thing is needed. Mary has chosen what is better. And it will not be taken away from her."—Luke 10:41–42

Topic: Mary and Martha have a special dinner guest

Bible Exploration: Luke 10:38–42

Martha and Mary, who were sisters, lived in a city called Bethany. They both loved Jesus very much. When Jesus and His disciples came to Bethany, Martha invited them into her home. Jesus and His disciples accepted the invitation. Mary sat at Jesus's feet so that she would not miss a word He said, but Martha was busy preparing food for her guests. Martha was upset that she was working alone while Mary was enjoying herself. Finally Martha complained to

Jesus that it was not fair that she was having to do all the work while Mary just sat and listened.

Jesus loved both Martha and Mary and knew they were faithful followers. Jesus explained to Martha that she was worried about unimportant things. Martha was concerned about preparing food and was missing hearing words from Jesus, the Son of God. Jesus was letting Martha know that she needed to hear the Word of God. Jesus didn't want Martha doing things for Him instead of listening to Him. He also wants you not to be too busy to share your time with Him by praying, reading the Bible, and attending Bible study at church.

In the following activity, you will make a Bible scripture ring. Instead of writing the scriptures on the paper strips, you can type them on a computer and print them out on labels. You can use different-colored poster boards or you can add designs to the strips of paper if you wish.

—— SCRIPTURE RING ——

You Need   8½-by-11-inch (21.3-by-27.5-cm) sheet of poster board
scissors
paper hole punch
ruler
pen
1-inch (2.5-cm) ring binder

1. Fold the poster board in half twice, first from top to bottom, then from side to side.

2. Unfold the poster board and cut across each fold line to obtain four pieces.

3. Fold one of the pieces in half twice by first placing the short sides together, then folding again in the same direction.

4. Unfold and cut along each fold line to obtain four strips of poster board.

5. Use the ruler and the hole punch to measure and make a centered hole ½ inch (1.25 cm) from one of the short sides of each strip.

6. Write one of these scripture verses on one side of each strip and the scripture reference on the opposite side:

Front	Back
"Shout to the Lord with joy."	Psalm 98:4a
"Love your enemies."	Matthew 5:44b
"Be kind and tender to one another"	Ephesians 4:32a
"Do not worry about anything."	Philippians 4:6a

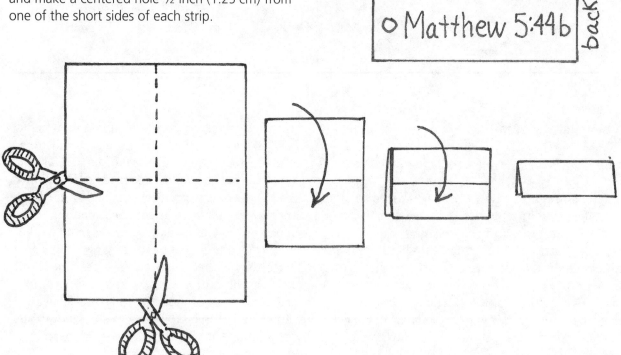

7. With all the scripture references facing up, stack the strips one on top of the other. Secure the strips by placing the ring binder through the holes.

8. Repeat steps 3 through 6 for each of the remaining three pieces of poster board. Use scripture verses of your choice. Open the ring and add these scripture strips to the collection formed in step 7.

9. Be like Mary and take time to listen to God's words and store them in your heart. Do this by reading and memorizing the scripture verses in your scripture ring. After a while, look at the reference and try to say the verse from memory.

—— Memory Verse ——

I spend time thinking about Your rules. I consider how You want me to live. (Psalm 119:15)

—— Think about This ——

The Lord's teachings and rules are written in the Bible. What are some of the Lord's rules that help you know how the Lord wants you to live?

[27] Returning Home

So he got up and went to his father. While the son was still a long way off, his father saw him. He was filled with tender love for his son. He ran to him. He threw his arms around him and kissed him.—Luke 15:20

Topic: The prodigal son
Bible Exploration: Luke 15:11–32

Jesus was speaking to a group and told a **parable** (a fictional story used to explain something) of a father and his two sons. Jesus wanted those hearing the story to understand that they had a father in heaven who would always be there for them no matter what happened or what they did, and they would always be His children.

The younger son decided to leave home and asked his father for his inheritance. The father was sad about this, but he divided his money and gave the younger son his share. At first the son had lots of fun. He bought many things and had lots of friends to spend his money on. Soon he ran out of money and discovered that the people he thought were his friends only liked him for his money.

During that time there was a famine in the land. There wasn't a lot of food, and jobs were hard to find. The son finally got the most unthinkable job for a Jew: feeding pigs. The pigsty was muddy and smelly, and the food he fed the pigs was slimy and gross. Soon the son was so hungry that the pigs' food was beginning to look good to him. He came to his senses and thought about his home. Because of the way he had treated his father, he thought that he did not deserve to be called his father's son. But he also thought that maybe he could return and work for his father as a hired helper, since his father gave his helpers plenty to eat.

So the son decided to go home. His father saw him and ran out to meet him. The father hugged and kissed his son and held him in his arms. The son told his father that he was not worthy to be his son, but the father was so excited to have his son home that he didn't listen. Instead he had his servants bring his son new clothes, and he put a ring on his son's finger as a sign that he was forgiven and was a part of the fam-

ily again. The father prepared a big party and invited everyone he knew to celebrate the return of his son.

While the father was happy about the son's return, the older son was jealous of the attention his younger brother was getting. After all, the older son thought, he had not run away and misbehaved. Why didn't the father give him a party and punish his brother? The father lovingly comforted this older son, explaining that he loved them both and that this was a time to rejoice. His younger son had been lost and now was found. Not only was the son home, he was a changed man. He left as a selfish son interested only in himself, and he returned home ready to be a hired hand just to be near his family again.

In the following activity, a dirty penny is cleaned to represent a change not only in the physical appearance of the prodigal son's body and clothes but a change in his attitude. New pennies are shiny, but being touched by dirty hands and being exposed to gases in the air make pennies dirty and dull. Soaking the pennies in a mixture of vinegar and salt removes the dull layer.

—— SHINY COIN ——

You Need
- ½ cup (125 mL) white vinegar
- two 10-ounce (300-mL) transparent plastic cups
- tap water
- ½ teaspoon (2.5 mL) salt
- spoon
- 2 dull pennies
- paper towel
- 3-by-5-inch (7.5-by-12.5-cm) unlined index card
- transparent tape
- pen

1. Pour the vinegar into one of the cups. Fill the other cup about half full with water.

2. Add the salt to the cup with the vinegar. Stir the mixture with the spoon.

3. Drop one of the pennies into the cup with the salt and vinegar.

4. Allow the coin to sit in the vinegar and salt mixture for 5 minutes.

5. Use the spoon to fish the penny out of the cup and place it into the cup of water. *CAUTION: If you get vinegar on your skin, rinse it thoroughly with water. Vinegar can burn the skin, especially if you have any cuts.*

6. You can use your fingers to take the penny out of the water, then dry it with the paper towel.

7. Lay the uncleaned penny and the cleaned penny side by side on the index card. Secure them with tape. Write "Before" under the dirty penny and "After" under the cleaned penny.

8. Display the card in your room to remind you of the changes in the prodigal son's appearance and attitude.

— Memory Verse —

Lord, You are good. You are forgiving. You are full of love for all who call out to You. (Psalm 86:5)

— Think about This —

The prodigal son wished he had not left home. Have you ever done something that you wished you had not done? Did you admit to what you did and ask to be forgiven?

28 Never Give Up!

Jesus told His disciples a story. He wanted to show them that they should always pray and not give up.—Luke 18:1

Topic: The persistent widow
Bible Exploration: Luke 18:1–8

Jesus told a parable to teach His disciples that they should always pray and not give up. The story is about a widow who went to a judge seeking justice. But the judge would not help her. The judge was a man who cared neither about God nor about what people thought of him. The widow knew she was right and was determined that the judge give her justice. She continued to go to the judge, saying, "Give me my rights!" After a long time, the judge gave the woman her rights. The woman's persistence did not change the judge's heart. He continued to

say that he did not care about God or about what people thought of him. But he gave the widow justice, not because he wanted to do what was right in the sight of God or people but because he was so tired of being bothered by her.

Jesus explained that even the bad judge did what was right. He continued by saying that God will always do what is right for His people, and unlike the bad judge, He will not be slow to answer. The story was told to stress that if an ungodly man will listen to someone who is persistent, how much more will a loving God listen to the prayers of His people? Does this mean that if you keep asking God for something He will finally give it to you? No. In the story, Jesus said that God knows what is right for you. When you pray, you can depend on a speedy answer from God. He answers in three ways: "Yes," "No," or "Wait."

In the following activity, you will make a paper prayer chain. Red and white paper is described, but you can make the chain from any colored paper or from white paper that you color and decorate. You can include the names of people at school, in your family, and in your church.

— PRAYER CHAIN —

You Need 2 sheets of construction paper
        (1 red and 1 white)
        scissors
        pen
        transparent tape

1. Fold the red sheet of construction paper in half three times along the short side.

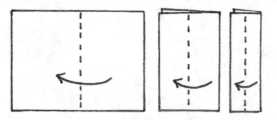

2. Unfold the paper and cut along all of the fold lines. You will have 16 red strips.

3. Repeat steps 1 and 2 using the white paper.

4. Write the names of family and friends on each of the strips.

5. Take a red strip and slightly overlap the ends. Secure the ends together with tape.

6. Take a white strip, run it through the red loop, and tape its ends together.

7. Repeat step 6, but add a red strip, then a white strip, until all but one strip is used.

8. Run the last strip through the loops in both ends of the chain. Then tape the ends of the strip together. The chain can be worn as a necklace.

9. When you are not wearing the chain, hang it in your room. Whether you're wearing it or it's hanging in your room, the chain will be a reminder to pray for those whose names are written on the links.

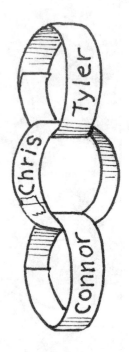

— Memory Verse —

Ask, and it will be given to you. Search, and you will find. Knock, and the door will be opened to you. (Matthew 7:7)

— Think about This —

Jesus knew that people are not always sure what they should pray for. This is why He taught His disciples to ask, search, and knock. This lesson was an encouragement to keep on praying. Do you pray only when you want something? Do you ever pray just to thank God for what you have?

29 Childlike Faith

Jesus said, "Let the little children come to Me. Don't keep them away. The kingdom of heaven belongs to people like them."—Matthew 19:14

Topic: Jesus welcomes children
Bible Exploration: Matthew 19:13–15; Mark 10:13–16

Jesus was busy traveling from place to place teaching the Word of God and healing people. Wherever He was, there was always a crowd of people asking questions and hoping to be healed. His disciples were very helpful, but one day parents tried to bring their little children forward so that Jesus could lay His hands on them and pray for them. The disciples refused to let the parents bring the children to Jesus.

They may have thought Jesus was too busy to be bothered with little children. But Jesus was never too busy to make little children feel welcome. He used the children to teach His disciples and others about the importance of having a childlike faith.

Little children are loving and trusting. Those with childlike faith are eager and alert—eager to invite others to know more about Jesus and alert to the needs of others.

In the following activity, you will make a paper airplane. It shows that the child drawn on the plane has faith that the plane will keep him or her aloft.

You Need   sheet of white copy paper
                pencil
                crayons or colored markers
                paper clip

1. Fold the paper in half by placing the long sides together, then unfold the paper.

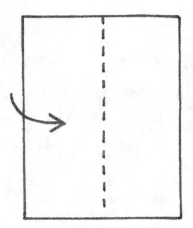

2. Fold the top edges, A and B, to the center crease.

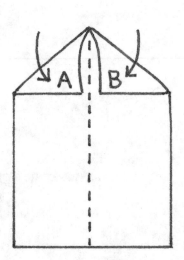

3. Fold the paper in half again along the center fold line. Crease with the folded corners inside.

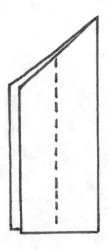

4. Fold one side down so that it touches the folded edge as shown. Press the folded side with your fingers to make it flat.

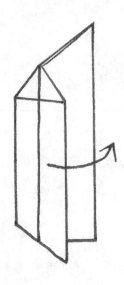

5. Use the pencil to draw the outline of a child so that the center of the figure is along the center fold line of the paper.

6. Add hair, eyes, and other features to the figure. Add clothes that represent a boy or a girl. Then, using crayons, color the figure.

7. Repeat step 4, folding the other side.

8. Lift each of the folded sides so that they are perpendicular to the body of the airplane that has been formed.

9. Attach a paper clip to the front end of the airplane.

10. Hold the airplane from below and throw it to make it fly through the air.

11. Show the airplane to friends and explain that the child drawing represents faith that airplanes can carry us through the air. It is also a reminder to have faith in Jesus.

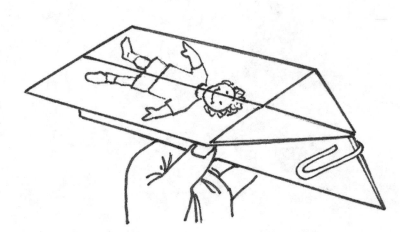

— Memory Verse —

So faith comes from hearing the message. And the message that is heard is the word of Christ. (Romans 10:17)

— Think about This —

Are you eager to share what you know about Jesus with others? How can you tell a friend about Jesus?

30 New Sight

Right away he could see. He followed Jesus, praising God.
When all the people saw it, they also praised God.—Luke 18:43

Topic: Bartimaeus's faith heals him
Bible Exploration: Luke 18:35–43

Bartimaeus was a blind beggar whom Jesus met on the road outside Jericho. Jesus and His disciples were on their way to Jerusalem with a great crowd of people following them. Bartimaeus could hear the voices of the people. When he learned that Jesus was part of the group, he began to cry out to Jesus. He wanted Jesus to heal him. People in the crowd told Bartimaeus to be quiet. But he cried even louder. Jesus stopped and asked for Bartimaeus to be brought to Him. Jesus asked Bartimaeus, "What do you want me to do for you?" Bartimaeus said he wanted to see. Jesus told Bartimaeus he would be healed and receive his sight because of his faith. Immediately Bartimaeus could see.

Bartimaeus trusted that Jesus had the power to make him see. His faith in Jesus was so strong that he continued to cry out to Jesus for help even though people around him tried to make him stop. Jesus responded to Bartimaeus's faith and healed him.

When blind, Bartimaeus saw only darkness. After Jesus came into his life, Bartimaeus not only had new sight but a new life—he was a follower of Jesus.

In the following activity, you will compare a black picture with a multicolored one to see the difference between Bartimaeus's life before and after finding Jesus.

You Need   6-by-16-inch (15-by-40-cm) piece of white poster board
marker
black, red, yellow, and blue liquid poster paints

1. Fold the poster board in half so that the short edges meet.

2. Fold each short edge back toward the fold into an accordion shape.

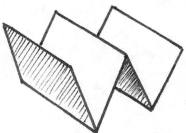

3. Unfold the poster board, then use the marker to write "Without Jesus" at the top of the first section and "With Jesus" at the top of the third section.

4. Place one pea-size blob of black paint in the center of the first fold. Place another blob of black paint of equal size about ½ inch (1.25 cm) below the first blob.

5. Fold the first section of the poster board over the second section. Then use your fingers to spread the paint inside by pressing and rubbing the poster board.

6. Unfold the poster board.

7. Repeat steps 4 and 5 using one blob each of red, yellow, and blue, but place the blobs in the fold between the third and fourth sections.

8. Allow the paint to dry.

9. Slightly bend the poster board along the fold lines so that it will stand upright. Stand the poster board in your room to remind you of the change that Jesus made in Bartimaeus's life as well as in yours. When friends ask you about the black and the colored pictures, you can tell them the story of Jesus and Bartimaeus.

—— Memory Verse ——

The Lord gives sight to those who are blind. The Lord lifts up those who feel helpless. The Lord loves those who do what is right. (Psalm 146:8)

—— Think about This ——

The Lord gave sight to Bartimaeus. What has the Lord done for you?
How can you increase your faith in Jesus?

[31] Up a Tree

So he ran ahead and climbed a sycamore-fig tree. He wanted to see Jesus, who was coming that way.—Luke 19:4

Topic: Zacchaeus tries to see Jesus
Bible Exploration: Luke 19:1–10

Jesus had come to the city of Jericho, where Zacchaeus lived. Zacchaeus was rich because he was a dishonest tax collector. He was trying to see who Jesus was, but because he was short, Zacchaeus could not see over the crowd. He ran ahead and climbed a tree to see Jesus when He passed by.

Jesus looked up and told Zacchaeus to hurry down from the tree because He was going to his house. The people in the crowd heard this and became angry because Jesus was going to the house of a thief. They didn't understand that Jesus had come to look for and save the lost.

(A **lost** person doesn't know that Jesus is his or her Savior. A **saved** person is someone who knows that Jesus is his or her Savior. For more information about being saved, see chapter 36, "The Greatest Gift.")

As a saved person, Zacchaeus was a changed man. He vowed not only to give away half of his wealth to the poor but also to repay anyone he had cheated. Jesus was happy about the changes in Zacchaeus's behavior.

In the following activity, you will make a tree to remind you of how Zacchaeus met Jesus and was saved. The cardboard tube can be an empty toilet paper tube, or you can cut a piece from an empty paper towel tube.

⸺ ZACHAEUS'S TREE ⸺

You Need
- 6-by-6-inch (15-by-15-cm) piece of white copy paper
- brown, light green, and dark green crayons
- 4-inch (10-cm) empty cardboard tube
- transparent tape
- scissors
- pencil
- 6-by-6-inch (15-by-15-cm) piece of white poster board

1. Lay the piece of copy paper against the bark of a tree and rub the brown crayon back and forth across the entire piece of paper. You will have made a bark rubbing.

2. Place the bark rubbing side of the paper down on a table, then place the cardboard tube in the center of the paper.

3. Wrap the paper around the tube and secure it with tape. This is the tree trunk.

4. Fold the ends of the paper over and tuck them into the tube at each end.

5. Cut two slits, each about 1 inch (2.5 cm) long, opposite each other on one end of the paper tube.

6. Use the pencil to draw the tree shape on the poster board as shown. Then cut out the drawing.

7. Use the green crayon to color the tree shape a light green. Then color the leaves a darker green.

8. Insert the tree shape into the cuts on the tree trunk.

9. Stand the tree in your room to remind you that nothing should stop you from trying to see Jesus. Zacchaeus had to climb a tree to do this, but you can find Jesus by praying and reading your Bible.

⸺ Memory Verse ⸺

The Son of Man came to look for the lost and save them. (Luke 19:10)

⸺ Think about This ⸺

Zacchaeus's life changed when he met Jesus.
How can you encourage others to know about Jesus?

32 The Vine and the Branches

"I am the vine. You are the branches. If anyone remains joined to Me, and I to him, he will bear a lot of fruit. You can't do anything without Me."—John 15:5

Topic: Staying connected to Jesus
Bible Exploration: John 15:1–8

Jesus told His 12 disciples that He would soon leave Earth and join God the Father in heaven. Even after He was gone, Jesus assured His disciples that they could continue to be guided and strengthened by Him. To help them understand how this could happen, He compared Himself to a vine and the disciples to its branches.

Jesus told the disciples that they would receive what they needed to bear **spiritual fruit** (thoughts and behavior that glorify God) if they would remain joined to Him. With this fruit, they could continue to complete the job Jesus had given them, which was

to encourage others to become His followers.

Jesus spoke face-to-face with the 12 disciples just as He speaks to His followers today through His words in the Bible. Followers who are joined to Jesus produce spiritual fruit that prepares them to encourage others to trust and believe in Jesus.

In the following activity, a paper loop represents being joined to Jesus. You will start with a prepared loop of paper. The loop is cut in half, but it does not divide into two parts. Instead a loop that is twice as big around is formed. Your name and the name of Jesus are on the larger loop, representing that you are still joined to Jesus. The increased size of the loop represents an increase in your spiritual fruit.

You Need   2-by-36-inch (5-by-90-cm) piece of
adding machine tape (any unpatterned paper will work)
marker
scissors
transparent tape

1. Lay the paper strip on a table and draw a line as straight as possible down the center of the paper as shown.

2. Using the markers, print "Jesus" on one side of the line and print your name on the other side in large letters.

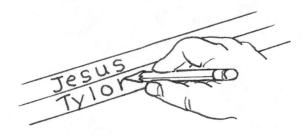

3. Holding the ends of the strip, add a twist to the paper by turning one end 180 degrees (one-half of a full turn), then tape the ends together to make a closed loop. Make sure the tape covers the width of the paper strip.

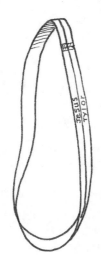

4. On the loop where the edges are taped together, fold the strip, then cut a slit about 2 inches (5 cm) long across the fold and along the line drawn on the paper.

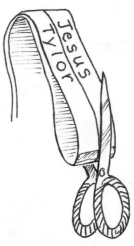

5. Insert the scissors into the slit in the paper loop and cut along the line all the way around the loop. The paper will open up, forming one large loop.

6. You can repeat this activity for a friend. Prepare the paper loop in advance, writing your friend's name on the paper instead of yours. After the loop has been cut, you can explain how it represents being joined to Jesus and the results.

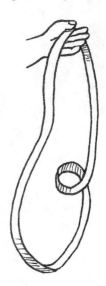

⟶ Memory Verse ⟵

But anyone who is joined to the Lord becomes one with Him in spirit.
(1 Corinthians 6:17)

⟶ Think about This ⟵

What are the results of being joined to Jesus?

33 Three Times

Then Peter remembered what Jesus had said. "The rooster will crow," Jesus had told him. "Before it does, you will say three times that you don't know Me." Peter went outside. He broke down and sobbed.—Matthew 26:75

Topic: Peter's three denials
Bible Exploration: Matthew 26:34–35, 69–75

Jesus and His 12 disciples gathered together in Jerusalem to celebrate **Passover**. This is a yearly Jewish holiday that is a reminder of the last night the Israelites were slaves in Egypt, when the angel of death passed over the houses of those who followed the instructions that God gave to Moses.

During Passover, there is one special meal when families celebrate together and retell the story of how God delivered the Israelite slaves from Egypt. When Jesus and His disciples joined together for the Passover meal, Jesus told

them that He would die soon and that they would all deny that they were His followers. Peter said that he would never deny being Jesus's follower. Jesus told Peter that he would deny Him three times before a rooster crowed the next morning.

Jesus was right. All the disciples denied Him. Because Peter was afraid of what would happen to him, he denied knowing Jesus three times before the morning came and a rooster crowed. When he heard the rooster crow, Peter remembered what Jesus had said and was sad. It was a lesson for Peter, and from then on he became a bold witness for Jesus. A **witness** is a person who tells what he or she has seen or knows to be the truth. Peter spent the remainder of his life telling others the Good News, which is that Jesus Christ is the Son of God and that He died for their sins.

In the following activity, you will change a paper cup into a noisemaker that sounds like a rooster. Both hens and roosters make clucking sounds, but only roosters crow. With practice, you can make the noisemaker cluck and crow.

ROOSTER SOUNDS

You Need
16-ounce (480-mL) yellow plastic cup
black permanent marker
ice pick (a hammer and a nail will work)
    CAUTION: Adult use only
12-inch (30-cm) piece of string
2-by-1-inch (5-by-2.5-cm) piece of dish-
    washing sponge
tap water
adult helper

1. Turn the cup upside down, and using the marker, draw eyes and a bird's beak on the cup as shown.

2. Ask an adult to use the ice pick to make two holes about 1 inch (2.5 cm) apart in the center of the bottom of the cup.

3. Thread one end of the string through the holes and tie it on the outside of the cup as shown.

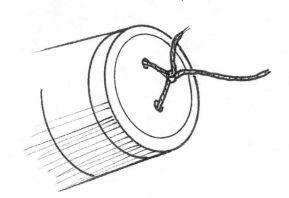

4. Tie the other end of the string around the center of the piece of sponge.

5. Wet the sponge with water, then squeeze as much water as possible out of it. You want the sponge moist but not dripping wet.

6. Hold the cup in one hand and wrap the wet sponge around the string as close to the cup as possible. Pressing the sponge against the string, pull the sponge down the string in a jerky motion. A loud sound much like that of a clucking rooster will be heard. Change the motion of pulling the sponge down the string until more of a crowing sound is heard.

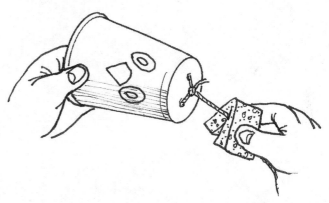

7. The rooster sounds will be a reminder to be a bold witness for Jesus.

—— Memory Verse ——

What about someone who says in front of others that he knows Me? I will also say in front of My Father who is in heaven that I know Him. (Matthew 10:32)

—— Think about This ——

What you say is one way to share Jesus's love. What are some of the ways that you share the love of Jesus with others?

34 The Rescue Plan

But here is how God has shown His love for us.
While we were still sinners, Christ died for us.—Romans 5:8

Topic: Jesus died for our sins
Bible Exploration: Genesis 4:16; Mark 15:33–34; John 18 and 19; Romans 3:23, 5:6–11, 6:23; 2 Peter 2:4–6

The Bible is like a jigsaw puzzle with every verse being a puzzle piece. Each puzzle piece is important and needed. But you get more out of each piece when they are connected. Likewise, each verse in the Bible is very important, but also like a jigsaw puzzle, you get more out of each verse when the verses are connected.

It is easier to put jigsaw pieces together if you look at the picture on the puzzle box. It is also easier to understand the Bible if you know that

it forms a picture of God's love. So if you read what seems to be a scary part, read on because God's love will be revealed when more verses are connected. For example, verses in Genesis explain that the penalty for sin is spiritual death (separation from God). Romans 3:23 says everyone has sinned. So everyone is guilty and has received a death sentence. But when more verses are added, God's rescue plan is revealed. In this plan, the penalty for sin doesn't change, and God demands payment. But a Savior, Jesus Christ, pays the penalty for your sins.

The part of the Bible revealing Jesus paying this penalty shows Him dying on a cross. This part makes us sad, but we can be thankful that

He loved us so much that He suffered and died for us. For the gloriously happy part of God's rescue plan, see chapter 35, "The Easter Story."

In the following activity, you will use a sheet of paper to form the shape of the cross. The cross will represent a Bible puzzle piece showing God's rescue plan. You can use white or colored copy paper.

~ THE CROSS ~

You Need   Sheet of copy paper

1. Fold the paper so that side A touches side B. Crease the fold by pressing it with your fingers.

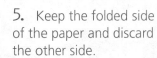
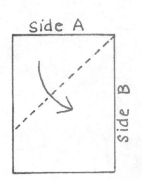

2. Fold the paper so that corner B touches corner A. Crease the fold.

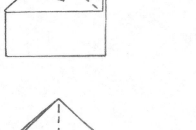

3. Fold the paper in half as shown. Crease the fold.

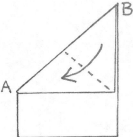

4. Starting at the bottom of the folded paper at a point about 1 inch (2.5 cm) from the folded edge (marked by the arrow), tear across the paper as shown.

5. Keep the folded side of the paper and discard the other side.

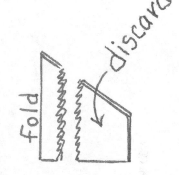

6. Unfold the paper. A cross is formed.

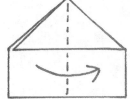

7. Show friends how to make a cross, then tell them how it was part of God's rescue plan.

~ Memory Verse ~

God loved the world so much that He gave His one and only Son. Anyone who believes in Him will not die but will have eternal life. (John 3:16)

~ Think about This ~

Why did Jesus die on the cross?

35 The Easter Story

"He is not here! He has risen, just as He said He would!
Come and see the place where He was lying."—Matthew 28:6

Topic: Christ rises from the dead
Bible Exploration: Matthew 27:57–66,
28:1–15

Jesus loves us so much that He died on the cross
to pay the penalty for our sins. After He died,
His body was placed in a tomb owned by a man
named Joseph of Arimathea. At this time, a
tomb was a cave in which people were buried.
A large stone was placed over the opening of the
tomb. Priests and other Jewish leaders went to
Pilate, the Roman governor. They told Pilate
that Jesus had said before He was killed that He
would rise from the dead in three days. They
suggested that Jesus's followers might steal the

body and claim that Jesus had risen from the
dead. They asked Pilate to have the tomb
guarded, and he did.

On the third day after Jesus's death, two
women, both named Mary, went to the grave.
They were surprised to see the stone rolled
away and an angel sitting on it. The angel told
the women not to be afraid and that Jesus was
not there because He had risen from the dead.
The angel invited them to look inside the tomb.
Then he told them to go quickly and tell the disciples that Jesus had risen from the dead and
was alive.

Easter is a Christian holiday that marks the
day when God raised Jesus from the dead. It

is a day of thanksgiving for Jesus's sacrifice and a day of celebration that Jesus rose from the dead so that Christians can have **eternal life**.

In the following activity, you will create a surprising picture to remind you of the surprise that Jesus was alive. The black outline of the figures can be seen through the red plastic, but the pink, orange, and yellow colors are not visible. The red plastic acts as a filter to block these colors. Before using the highlighters, test them to make sure the plastic blocks out the color of their ink. Do this by marking on a sheet of white paper with each pen. Then place the red plastic over the marks. If any mark is visible through the plastic, do not use the highlighter that made that mark. Instead, try another type of highlighter of the same color, but test it first.

——— SURPRISE ART ———

You Need   copy of envelope pattern (see the next page)
pencil
ruler
scissors
transparent tape
black pen
pink, orange, and yellow fluorescent highlighters
4-by-4-inch (10-by-10-cm) piece of red transparent plastic (cut the piece from a red plastic report folder)

1. Make a photocopy of the envelope pattern.

2. Cut out the envelope, then cut out the window.

3. Fold the envelope along the center fold line.

4. Fold tab A over side A and secure with tape. Repeat with tab B.

5. Use the pen to draw an Easter picture inside the envelope window, such as the one shown.

6. Use the highlighters to color the picture.

7. Slide the red plastic into the envelope so that it covers the picture. Note that the colors seem to disappear.

8. You can use this surprise picture to tell your friends about the amazing story of Jesus rising from the dead. First show them the picture through the red plastic. Then pull out the plastic to reveal the whole picture. Once your friends have been surprised, tell them that you keep the picture to remind you of the biggest surprise ever, which was Jesus rising from the dead.

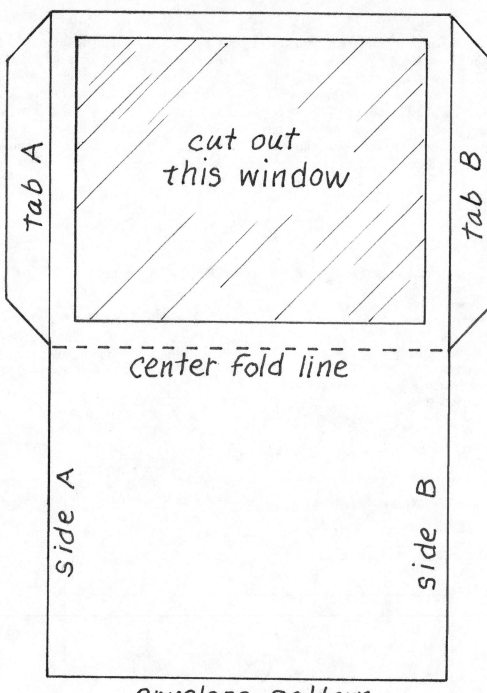

tab A

cut out
this window

tab B

- - - center fold line - - -

side A

side B

envelope pattern

—— Memory Verse ——

He was buried. He was raised from the dead on the third day, just as Scripture said He would be. (1 Corinthians 15:4)

—— Think about This ——

What is the meaning of Easter?

36 The Greatest Gift

But God loves us deeply. He is full of mercy. So He gave us new life because of what Christ has done. He gave us life even when we were dead in sin. God's grace has saved you. —Ephesians 2:4

Topic: Salvation

Bible Exploration: Luke 1:77; John 3:16; Acts 4:12, 13:26–32; Titus 3:3–7

A **gift** is something special given by one person to another. The greatest gift anyone can receive is God's grace. **Grace** is the love, kindness, and forgiveness of God shown to someone who has done nothing to deserve it. God's grace is the reason you have been given a pardon for all your sins, which means that all your sins—past, present, and future—have been forgiven.

Salvation is believing in God's saving grace. God's grace is not given because of anything believers have done. Instead it is God's gift.

In the following activity, you will make an **acrostic**, which is a a list of words or phrases in which the first letter of each line forms a word. The word it forms is *grace*.

You Need   marker
ruler
sheet of white copy paper
crayons

1. Using the marker and the ruler, print the letters G, R, A, C, and E down the paper about 2 inches (5 cm) from the left edge as shown.

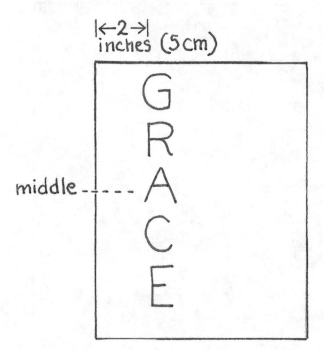

3. Use crayons to add crosses and/or the Christian fish symbol, as shown.

2. Using the marker, write in the words for each line listed here:

God's
Rescue
At
Christ's
Expense

4. Display the acrostic to remind you of God's greatest gift, grace.

5. Make more acrostics to give to friends. Explain that because of God's grace, He sent Jesus to die for their sins and He raised Jesus from death so that they will live forever with Him in heaven.

--- Memory Verse ---

We have been set free because of what Christ has done. Through His blood our sins have been forgiven. We have been set free because God's grace is so rich.
(Ephesians 1:7)

--- Think about This ---

What are the three parts in God's gift of grace?

37 A Helper

"If you love Me, you will obey what I command. I will ask the Father, and He will give you another Friend to help you and to be with you forever. The Friend is the Spirit of truth. The world can't accept Him. This is because the world does not see Him or know Him. But you know Him. He lives with you, and He will be in you." John 14:15–17

Topic: Jesus promises another helper
Bible Exploration: Acts 1:6–11; Mark 13:32; Luke 12:1; John 15:26–27; Acts 1:8; Ephesians 1:13–14

When Jesus was on Earth, He was His disciples' closest Friend, and they depended on Him for help and comfort. Before Jesus returned to heaven, He promised that another Friend just like Him would come. This Friend is God the Holy Spirit.

After Jesus was lifted up to heaven, the Holy Spirit came as promised. He is part of all Christians today. He is always there to guide and direct them. With the help of the Holy Spirit, Christians can better do God's work. When they read the Bible, the Holy Spirit helps them understand what they have read.

The Bible uses the word **fruit** to describe the outward evidence of what is in our heart. So the fruit of the Holy Spirit can only be produced by those who have the Holy Spirit in their heart. The fruit of the Holy Spirit is love, joy, peace, faith, gentleness, self-control, kindness, goodness, and patience. When a believer is totally living by the Holy Spirit's power, he or she produces all of the fruit. See chapter 41, "Choose Your Leader," to see what you can do to be led by the power of the Holy Spirit.

In the following activity, you will make a mobile showing the fruit of the Holy Spirit.

— FRUIT MOBILE —

You Need
yardstick (meterstick)
pen
22-by-22-inch (55-by-55-cm) piece of
   poster board
scissors
transparent tape
marker
5 index cards
ruler
string

1. Use the yardstick (meterstick) and the pen to draw two diagonal lines across the poster board square. To make the poster board easier to fold along these lines, press against it firmly with the pen.

2. Fold the poster board square along one of the diagonal lines. Crease the fold by pressing it flat with your fingers.

3. Unfold the paper and fold along the other diagonal line. Crease the fold.

4. Cut up one of the folds to the center of the paper, forming triangles A and B, as shown in the diagram.

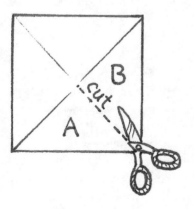

5. Overlap triangle B with triangle A and secure them together with tape. A pyramid is formed.

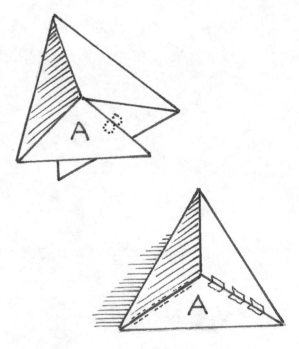

6. Use the marker to label each of the three sides of the pyramid "Christian Fruit."

7. Fold each index card in half by placing the short sides together. Unfold the cards and cut across the fold line. Keep nine of the cards and discard the extra one.

8. Use the pen to write the nine fruits of the spirit on the cards, one on each card: Love, joy, peace, faith, gentleness, self-control, kindness, goodness, and patience.

9. Measure and cut nine 6-inch (15-cm) pieces of string.

10. Use tape to secure one end of a piece of string to one of the fruit cards and the other to the edge of the pyramid. Repeat, hanging three cards from each side of the pyramid as shown.

11. Decide where you will hang the mobile.

12. Measure and cut a piece of string long enough to hang the mobile. Attach the string to the top of the pyramid and hang it where you can see it. It will be a reminder to keep God's Word stored in your heart so that the fruit you grow is the fruit of the Holy Spirit.

— Memory Verse —

But the fruit the Holy Spirit produces is love, joy, and peace. It is being patient, kind, and good. It is being faithful and gentle and having control of oneself. (Galatians 5:22)

— Think about This —

Which fruit of the Holy Spirit did you produce today?

38 A Change of Direction

On his journey, Saul approached Damascus. Suddenly a light from heaven flashed around him. He fell to the ground. He heard a voice speak to him. "Saul! Saul!" the voice said. "Why are you opposing Me?"—Acts 9:3, 4

Topic: Saul's change of attitude
Bible Exploration: Acts 9:1–19

Saul was a very educated and very religious man. He studied the Law of God and went to the temple to worship God regularly. But Saul was not a **believer**—a follower of Jesus. He hated believers. Saul had the power to find believers and put them in prison or have them killed.

One day Saul and other men were traveling to Damascus to seek out believers. When they were near the town, suddenly a light from heaven flashed all around Saul. It startled Saul so much that he fell from his donkey to the ground. Then Saul heard a voice from heaven calling his name and asking why Saul was opposing Him. Saul was very afraid. He asked, "Who are you?" And the voice answered, "I am Jesus, the one you are opposing." Saul heard Jesus's words and for the first time understood that he was hurting Jesus by hurting Jesus's followers. Jesus told Saul to enter Damascus and someone there would tell him what to do. Saul got up from the ground, but he was blind. His men had to lead him to Damascus. For three days Saul remained blind. During this time he had a **vision** (a dream with a message from God). In the dream, a man placed his hands over Sauls' eyes, and his sight returned.

In Damascus, Ananias, a believer, also had a

vision. In his dream, the Lord told him where to find Saul and to go there to ask for Saul. The Lord also told Ananias about Saul's vision.

Ananias knew that Saul had come to Damascus to arrest believers. But the Lord said to Ananias, "Go! I have chosen this man to work for Me." Ananias obeyed. He explained to Saul that the Lord had sent him so that Saul could see again. Just as Saul had seen in his vision, Ananias placed his hands over Saul's eyes and a miracle happened. Immediately Saul's sight returned.

Saul's meetings with Jesus resulted in a change for Saul. Instead of hating believers, Saul was now a believer. Saul's new job was to encourage others to have a change of attitude and become believers. One group hearing Saul's message referred to the believers as **Christians**, and this name is used today.

In the following activity, a twirling piece of paper will be used to represent Saul's actions before and after he became a believer. Saul's actions before believing in Jesus—the wrong way—will be the counterclockwise direction of the twirling paper. To go from the wrong way to the right way, there was a change in Saul's life. This change was due to his meeting Jesus that resulted in his believing the truth that Jesus is Lord of his life. This is represented by the change in the position of the paper flaps. Changing the wings causes the paper to twirl in the opposite direction, which represents the right way.

—— TURN AROUND ——

You Need   scissors
             2 paper clips

1. Make a photocopy of the twirler pattern on the next page.

2. Cut out the twirler, cutting around the outside as well as along the line between the flaps.

3. Bend the flap labeled "Right Way" forward, the flap labeled "Wrong Way" in the opposite direction, and crease along the fold line. The flap labeled "Wrong Way" should be facing up.

4. Attach the paper clips together, forming a two-link chain. Then attach the paper clip chain to the center of the twirler's tail.

5. Support the paper by holding the body beneath the bent flaps so that the body is vertical. Then use your other hand to lift the flaps up, slightly unfolding them. The flaps should be close to being perpendicular to the body. If the body is vertical, the flaps should be horizontal.

6. While holding the body in a vertical position, lift the paper as high as possible, then drop it. Notice that it twirls in a counterclockwise direction.

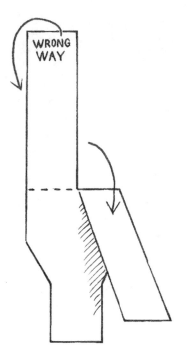

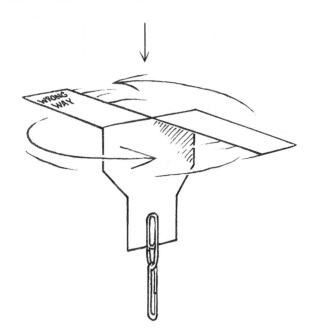

7. Repeat steps 3 through 6, folding the flaps in the opposite direction. This time the flap labeled "Right Way" will be facing up, and the paper will twirl in a clockwise direction.

8. You can have fun showing the paper twirler to friends. Explain what the labels on the flaps mean, and tell them about how Saul's life changed when he met Jesus.

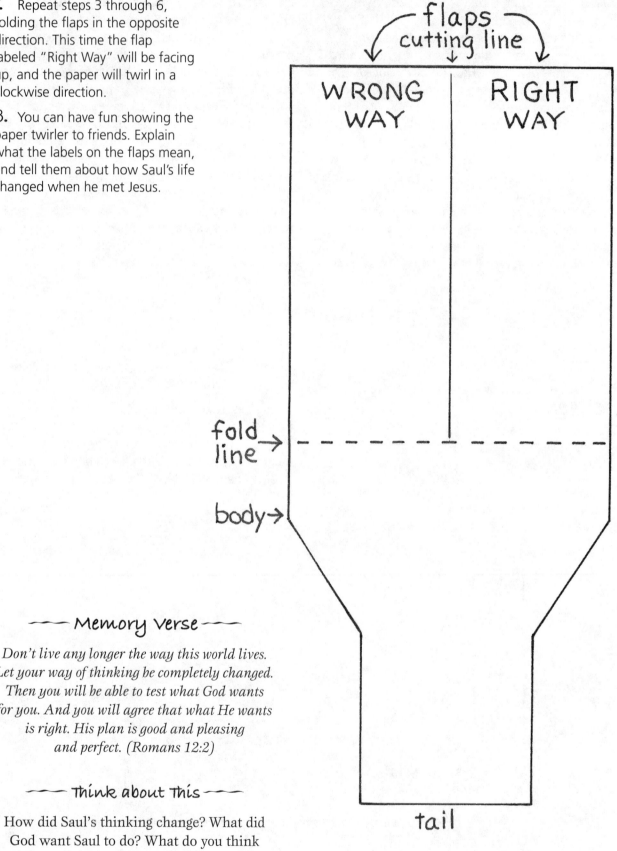

flaps
cutting line

WRONG WAY   RIGHT WAY

fold line →

body →

tail

—— Memory Verse ——

Don't live any longer the way this world lives. Let your way of thinking be completely changed. Then you will be able to test what God wants for you. And you will agree that what He wants is right. His plan is good and pleasing and perfect. (Romans 12:2)

—— Think about This ——

How did Saul's thinking change? What did God want Saul to do? What do you think God wants you to do?

39 Breakout

Suddenly an angel of the Lord appeared. A light shone in the prison cell. The angel struck Peter on his side. Peter woke up. "Quick!" the angel said. "Get up!" The chains fell off Peter's wrists.—Acts 12:7

Topic: An angel helps Peter escape from prison
Bible Exploration: Acts 12:1–19

King Herod did not like Christians. He had some Christians put in prison, and many of them were killed. Peter was in prison for telling others about Jesus. His friends were praying for his release. Peter was chained between two soldiers, and there were guards watching the door. God answered the prayers of Peter's friends and sent an angel to help Peter. The angel told Peter to get up and follow him. Peter's chains fell off, and he followed the angel. Peter and the angel walked past the sleeping soldiers and guards

and out of the prison. Peter escaped so that he could continue to tell others about Jesus.

In the following activity, the rubber band first moves back and forth just as Peter did before he was arrested. Twisting the second rubber band around your fingers represents the bars of the prison as well as the chains that bound Peter's hands and feet. It may seem that the twisted rubber band traps the other one. But, like Peter, the rubber band escapes. The rubber band escape is a trick, but Peter's escape was no trick—it was a miracle. Take off any rings you may be wearing before starting the activity.

── GREAT ESCAPE ──

You Need 2 thin rubber bands (The rubber bands must fit loosely around your fingers.)

1. Place one rubber band around your index and middle fingers as in position A.

position A

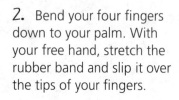

2. Bend your four fingers down to your palm. With your free hand, stretch the rubber band and slip it over the tips of your fingers.

3. Quickly snap your bent fingers up, pulling the tips out from under the rubber band. The rubber band will move from position A to position B, where it will be around your ring finger and little finger.

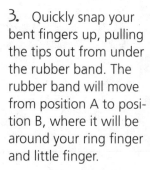

position B

4. Repeat steps 1 and 2 using your other hand to determine which hand works best for you. Once you decide on the best hand, repeat steps 1 and 2 until you can easily move the rubber band from one position to the other, then go to step 5.

5. Place the first rubber band around your fingers in position A (around your index and middle fingers). Place the second rubber band around the tip of your index finger and twist the rubber band so that one side crosses the other. Insert your middle finger in the opening and twist the rubber band again. Insert your ring finger in the space, twist the rubber band again, then insert your little finger into the space as shown.

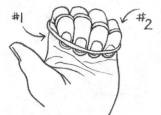

6. With rubber band 2 twisted around the ends of your fingers, repeat steps 2 and 3 to move rubber band 1 from position A to position B.

7. When you can easily perform this rubber band trick, show it to a friend. Have your friend stand in front of you so that he or she cannot see how you stretch the rubber band over your fingers. Start with two rubber bands as in step 5. Explain that rubber band 1 looped around two fingers represents Peter, and the twisted rubber band represents the chains and jail that confined Peter. Then repeat step 6. Explain that the escape of the rubber band represents Peter's escape from jail with the angel's help. You can show your friends the trick and encourage them to show it to others and to tell the story of how Peter's friends prayed and God sent an angel to free him.

── Memory Verse ──

My help comes from the Lord. He is the Maker of heaven and earth. (Psalm 121:2)

── Think about This ──

Peter needed help, and God sent an angel. Who has God sent to help you when you have needed help?

CHRISTIAN VALUES

40 Spiritual Food

I have hidden Your word in my heart so that I won't sin against You.—Psalm 119:11

Topic: Feeding your good nature
Bible Exploration: Psalms 37:31, 40:8, 119:11; Daniel 9:25; Luke 9:20

Christians have two natures: a good nature and a bad nature. Your **natures** are your behavior and thoughts. Your **good nature**, led by the desires of the Holy Spirit, wants only to please God. Your **bad nature**, led by your own desires, has no thoughts of pleasing God. The strength of each nature depends on how much you feed them. Feeding your two natures is much like feeding two plants. If you feed one plant but neglect the other one, the forgotten plant will get weak and wilt while the nourished plant will grow. Like the plants, the nature you nourish will grow and strengthen.

To nourish your good nature, you must feed it **spiritual food**, which is the Word of God. Plant food has to become a part of the plant for it to be used by the plant. Likewise, spiritual food has to become a part of you to make your good nature grow. You take in spiritual food by studying and memorizing God's Word. This is what hiding God's word in your heart means. The word **heart** is used in the Bible to mean the control center of all your thoughts and actions. With the Word in your heart, the Holy Spirit can help you to make the right choices so that you do not sin. He does this by bringing different verses to your remembrance.

Like a plant, which needs a daily supply of plant food, your good nature needs a daily supply of spiritual food, which is God's Word.

In the following activity, two celery stalks represent the results of feeding your good nature and neglecting to feed your bad nature.

⟶ GROWING GOOD NATURE ⟶

You Need   marker
two 1-quart (1-liter) plastic jars (large drinking glasses will work)
tap water
green food coloring
spoon
scissors
2 stalks of celery with pale green leaves (these are found in the inside of a celery bunch)
sheet of white copy paper
crayons

1. Use the marker to label one jar "Good Nature" and the other "Bad Nature."

2. Fill the jar labeled "Good Nature" with about 1 inch (2.5 cm) of water.

3. Add about 5 drops of food coloring to the water in the jar. Stir with the spoon until the water is one color. The colored water represents spiritual food.

4. Cut across the end of each celery stalk opposite the leaves.

5. Stand a celery stalk in each jar with the cut ends down.

6. Allow the jars to stand undisturbed for 2 days. Periodically compare how straight the stalks are and the color of their leaves. You will find that the

"Good Nature" celery continues to stand straight and its leaves get greener. The "Bad Nature" celery wilts and its leaves continue to be a pale green.

7. At the end of 2 days, use the paper and crayons to draw a picture of the jars and the celery stalks in them. You can display this picture to remind you to feed your good nature with God's Word. Share this activity with friends.

⟶ Memory Verse ⟶

"But suppose you suffer for being a Christian. Then don't be ashamed. Instead, praise God because you are known by that name." (1 Peter 4:16)

⟶ Think about This ⟶

What Bible verses do you know that help you when you are afraid or feeling sad?

Choose Your Leader

*The sinful nature does not want what the Spirit delights in.
And the Spirit does not want what the sinful nature delights in.
The two are at war with each other. That's what makes you
do what you don't want to do.—Galatians 5:17*

Topic: Be led by the holy spirit
Bible Exploration: Galatians 5:16–26;
Luke 6:43–45, 12:11; Romans 8:5

Christians have a good nature, also called a spirit nature. The characteristics of a Christian's spirit nature are called spiritual fruit. This fruit includes love, joy, peace, faith, gentleness, self-control, kindness, goodness, and patience. This fruit can only be produced by the power of the Holy Spirit. Christians also have a bad nature, also called a sinful nature. The Bible says the sinful nature and the Holy Spirit are at war with each other. This doesn't mean that they

fight and the winner takes over and controls you. Instead it means that the desires of each are opposite.

When people say, "The devil made me do it," they are saying that the devil took over and made them behave badly. But the Bible teaches that you can choose to be led by the desires of your sinful nature or by the Holy Spirit. When you choose to be led by the Holy Spirit, God uses His power to **activate** (to put into action) your desires that produce spiritual fruit.

In the following activity, baking powder represents your good nature and the vinegar the Holy Spirit's power. When they are combined, a chemical reaction occurs, producing a gas that causes foam. This change represents the Holy Spirit activating your desires and producing spiritual fruit. *CAUTION: If you get vinegar on your skin, rinse it thoroughly with water. Vinegar can burn the skin, especially if you have any cuts.*

—— ACTIVATED ——

You Need   marker
two 1-quart (1-liter) plastic jars (large drinking glasses will work)
1 teaspoon (5 mL) baking soda
¼ cup (63 mL) vinegar

1. Use the marker to label one jar "Good Nature" and the other "Holy Spirit Power."

2. Pour the baking soda into the jar labeled "Good Nature."

3. Pour the vinegar into the jar labeled "Holy Spirit Power."

4. With the baking soda and the vinegar in separate jars, nothing is happening.

5. To represent the activation of the good nature, pour the vinegar into the jar with the baking soda. *CAUTION: Be sure not to put a lid on the jar!*

6. Repeat this activity for a friend and explain that it represents the Holy Spirit (vinegar) activating their good desires (baking soda) and producing spiritual fruit (foam).

—— Memory Verse ——

So I say, live by the Holy Spirit's power. Then you will not do what your sinful nature wants you to do. (Galatians 5:16)

—— Think about This ——

How do you behave when you choose to be led by your sinful nature?
How do you behave when you choose to be led by the Holy Spirit?

⁴²⁾ Who Do You Serve?

"No one can serve two masters at the same time. He will hate one of them and love the other. Or he will be faithful to one and dislike the other. You can't serve God and Money at the same time."—Matthew 6:24

Topic: You cannot serve God and money
Bible Exploration: Matthew 6:19–24

A **slave** is controlled by something or someone. A **devoted** slave is one who is loyal and loving, which is demonstrated by giving your time, efforts, and attention. Jesus taught that we have a choice: we can either be a slave to God or a slave to money, but not to both at the same time. Trying to be devoted to God and to money at the same time is called being **double-minded**. A slave to money is devoted to the things that money can buy, such as clothes, toys, games,

and entertainment. This doesn't mean that it is wrong to want and have these things. But it means that things should not be more important to you than serving God.

Jesus taught that if you are devoted to money, you are storing treasures for yourself here on Earth. He said these treasures will not last. But if you are devoted to God, you are storing spiritual treasures in a heavenly storehouse, and these treasures will last forever.

In the following activity, you will discover how difficult it is to try to do two things at the same time. When a word that means a color is written in a different color, it is difficult to identify the color of the writing. That's because you automatically read the words that are printed. It takes more time to say the color because you have to concentrate harder. Your brain is trying to do two things, reading and identifying colors, but it can only do one thing at a time.

——DOUBLE-MINDED——

You Need   Red, blue, green, and yellow
              crayons
              sheet of white copy paper

1. Use the crayon color in parentheses to write the word preceding it.

    1.   Blue (red)

    2.   Pink (blue)

    3.   Black (yellow)

    4.   Purple (green)

    5.   Green (red)

    6.   Red (blue)

    7.   Brown (yellow)

    8.   Orange (green)

2. Place the paper, print side down, on a table.

3. Turn the paper over, and as quickly as possible, identify the color of each word in order, starting with number 1.

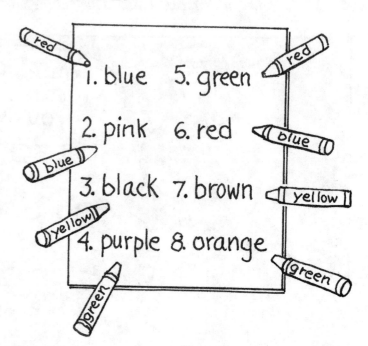

4. You can challenge friends by timing them to see who can accomplish the task the fastest. Don't forget to share that the activity demonstrates you cannot be double-minded when it comes to God. You are not to love anything as much or more than you love God.

—— Memory Verse ——

Your heart will be where your riches are. (Matthew 6:21)

—— Think about This ——

What kind of treasures are you storing?

[43] God Will Provide

"Look at the birds of the air. They don't plant or gather crops. They don't put away crops in storerooms. But your Father who is in heaven feeds them. Aren't you worth much more than they are?"—Matthew 6:26

Topic: Do not worry
Bible Exploration: Matthew 6:25–34

Worrying is being overly concerned about something. Jesus used birds and flowers as examples to teach that you should not worry. Why should you worry about where you are going to get food and clothing? God in heaven provides the food for birds. God doesn't drop birdseed from heaven. Instead He provides the rain, sunshine, and soil so that plants can grow and produce seeds for the birds to eat. God clothes the birds with beautiful feathers. God loves you much more than He loves birds, and He knows that you need food and clothing. The food and clothes that you need will not drop from the sky. As with the birds and the plants, God provides the resources to solve problems.

Jesus said that worrying is not going to change anything. Instead of worrying, He said to put God first in your life. If you are trusting in God and doing what He wants you to do, then the things you need will be given to you.

In the following activity, you will make a model of a growing flower to remind you that God provides for all of His creatures.

MORE AND MORE

You Need   14-by-28-inch (35-by-70-cm) piece of white poster board
crayons
black marker

1. Fold the poster board in half twice, folding the bottom edge over the top edge as shown.

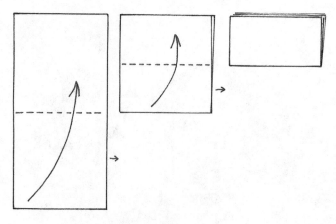

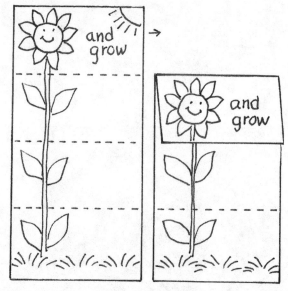

2. Unfold the poster board. Use crayons to draw a smiley-face flower on the left side, with the flower in the top section and the stem reaching from the top to the bottom section of the poster board. Add a sun, leaves, and grass as shown.

3. Use the marker to print the words "and grow" in the top right section of the poster board.

4. Fold the top section of the poster board down. Draw the same smiley-face flower with a stem that meets the stem on the third section as shown.

5. Print the words "and grow" at the top of the poster board with the marker.

6. Fold the top section of the poster board down. Draw a flower face and a stem as before. Then print the words "I don't worry! With God's care I grow" in the upper right side as shown.

7. Now unfold the poster board to make the flower appear to grow.

8. Show the growing flower to a friend. Explain that God takes care of flowers, and they grow and grow. Tell your friend that the growing flower is a reminder that God takes care of the flowers. He loves us more than flowers so He will take care of us, too.

— Memory Verse —

Turn all your worries over to Him. He cares about you. (1 Peter 5:7)

— Think about This —

What should you do when you feel worried?

44 It's Your Choice

The Holy Spirit led Jesus into the desert. There the devil tempted Him. After forty days and forty nights of going without eating, Jesus was hungry. The tempter came to Him. He said, "If You are the Son of God, tell these stones to become bread."—Matthew 4:1–3

Topic: Temptation
Bible Exploration: Matthew 4:1–11

When Jesus was on Earth, the devil tried to **tempt** Him, which means the devil tried to get Jesus to do something that was wrong. The devil chose a time when Jesus was physically weak. Jesus had been **fasting** (giving up food for a while during a time of prayer and worship to God). Jesus wanted to be ready to do what God wanted Him to do, so he fasted for 40 days. This made Him weak and very hungry. The devil said, "If you are the Son of God, tell these stones to become bread." The devil wanted Jesus to concentrate on His own need, which at the time was His hunger. So he tempted Jesus by challenging Him to prove He was the Son of God by using His power to make bread out of stone. The devil wanted Jesus to think about warm baked bread and how good it smells and tastes. Instead, Jesus responded to the devil with scripture. Even in His weakened condition, Jesus was able to resist temptation by using scripture to guide Him.

When you are tempted to do something that you know is wrong, such as not telling the truth or cheating in a game that you really want to win, *stop*, think about it, and ask yourself, "What would Jesus do?" You know that Jesus used scripture as a guide to make decisions. Like Jesus, you can be prepared to resist temptations by studying and memorizing God's word. The Bible also gives advice on how to avoid temptation.

In the following activity, some rice and a ball demonstrate that you can overcome any temptation with Christ's help. The ball in this jar represents a Christian and the rice kernels are temptations. When the ball is covered with the rice, it represents you when you are experiencing a temptation. When the jar is shaken, the rice kernels move around and get underneath the ball. As this settling of the rice continues, the ball is lifted to the surface. This represents you resisting the temptation. Just like the ball, with Christ's help you can always work your way out of tempting situations.

—— A WAY OUT——

You Need   1½ cups (375 mL) uncooked rice
1 quart (1 L) large-mouth plastic jar with lid
1 walnut-size rubber ball

1. Pour the rice into the jar.

2. Put the ball inside the jar and secure the lid.

3. Turn the jar over so that the ball falls to the bottom and is covered by the rice.

4. Shake the jar back and forth vigorously until the ball rises to the surface. *NOTE*: Do not shake the jar up and down.

5. Repeat steps 3 and 4 several times. Each time the ball will rise to the surface.

6. Demonstrate the rising ball to a friend. Start with the ball covered with rice so that your friend doesn't know what is in the jar. Then tell your friend to watch what happens when you shake the jar. Your friend will be surprised to see a ball that seems to magically appear. You can then share how the rice and the ball represent resisting temptation.

—— Memory Verse ——

I can do everything by the power of Christ.
He gives me strength. (Philippians 4:13)

—— Think about This ——

How can you be prepared to resist temptation?
What can you do to avoid temptation?

⌈45⌉ Soaring

But those who trust in the Lord will receive new strength.
They will fly as high as eagles. They will run and not get tired.
They will walk and not grow weak.—Isaiah 40:31

Topic: Gaining strength from God
Bible Exploration: Isaiah 40:29–31

It takes a lot of energy for a bird to fly. Birds would get too tired if they had to flap their wings all the time to stay afloat in the air. But God has given them the ability to soar, which means to move in the air without flapping their wings. They do this by extending their wings to catch rising warm air, which lifts them upward. So it is not the strength of the bird that is moving it upward; it is the strength of the rising air. While the bird is soaring, it is resting and gaining new strength.

If you do everything on your own, like the bird when it flaps its wings, you will get tired. But if you depend on the Lord, you can rest and gain new strength. This doesn't mean that you will be stronger so that you can lift heavy things; it means that you will have the power to resist temptation (doing wrong things). Also, instead of wearing yourself out by worrying about a problem, you will trust the Lord to solve it.

In the following activity, you will make a flying craft. The craft does not have a motor, so it has no energy of its own. It will fly only if you throw it. The craft depends on you for the energy needed to make it move. The craft should be thrown in an open outdoor area. Throw it in a direction away from other people.

You Need 3 or more different-colored permanent markers
large plastic lid, such as from a 39-ounce (1.1-kg) can of coffee (smaller plastic lids will also work)

1. Using one of the markers, write "Strength from God" on the plastic lid.

2. Use the markers to decorate the plastic lid. Draw an outdoor scene such as the one shown here with a bird soaring in the sky.

3. Allow the marker ink to dry for 3 to 5 minutes so that it will not smear when touched.

4. In an open outdoor area, throw the plastic lid in the same manner that you would throw a Frisbee. The lid should soar through the air.

5. Do the activity with a friend and explain that the flying lid is a reminder that Christians who depend on God for their strength have the power to resist temptation.

— **Memory Verse** —

Look to the Lord and to His strength. Always look to Him.
(1 Chronicles 16:11)

— **Think about This** —

Even if you are trying to follow God, sometimes things happen that make you sad or discouraged. But God still wants you to obey and trust that He will provide the strength you need. What causes you to feel discouraged? When you are discouraged, what should you do?

[46] True Love

"But here is what I tell you who hear Me. Love your enemies. Do good to those who hate you. Bless those who call down curses on you. And pray for those who treat you badly."—Luke 6:27–28

Topic: Love everyone
Bible Exploration: Mark 12:30–31;
Luke 6:27–36; 1 John 4:7–21

A dictionary describes *love* as liking and caring for someone very much. The Bible describes a different kind of love. This love comes from God. God's love for us is so great that He sent His Son to give His life to pay for our sins. God's love changes us.

Jesus was asked which is the most important of all the commandments, and He said the most important one is to love the Lord your God with all your heart, mind, soul, and strength. The second most important one is to love everyone as much as you love yourself. It is easy to love someone who loves you and is nice to you. But how can you love your enemies, who treat you badly? The source of this kind of love has to come from God.

Loving God and loving others goes together. You cannot do one without the other. When you are kind to others, especially someone who is rude or mean to you, you are showing how great and loving God is. This is because you are sharing God's love. You may never want to be best friends with your enemies, but you can have kind thoughts about them and treat them kindly if you love God and ask Him to help you share His love with them.

In the following activity, you will make a paper flower with a hidden message of love. The petals of the flower will be folded over. When you place the folded flower in water, the petals will open, revealing your secret message inside. The petals open because the paper absorbs the water, causing the paper to expand.

—— SECRET MESSAGE ——

You Need   sheet of white copy paper
pencil
scissors
pen
large bowl
tap water

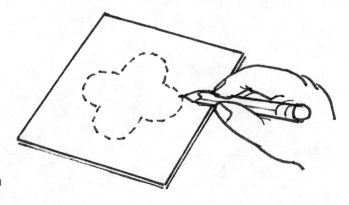

l.   Lay the paper over the flower pattern and trace the flower with the pencil.

2.   Cut the pattern from the paper.

3.   Use the pen to write a secret message, such as "I Love You" or "Welcome," in the center of the flower.

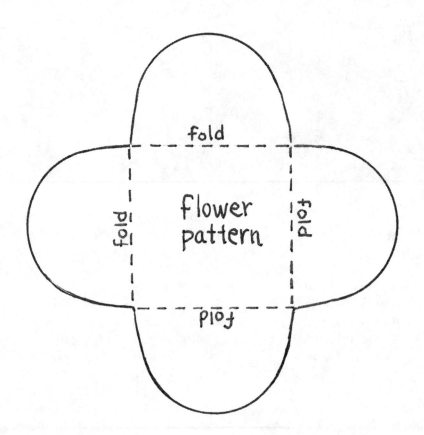

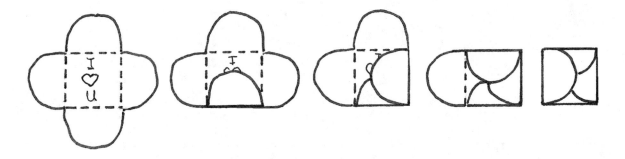

4. Fold the petals of the flower toward the center and crease them so that they lay flat. The petals will overlap.

5. Fill the bowl about half full with water.

6. Hold the folded paper, petal side up, about 4 inches (10 cm) above the bowl. Then drop the paper into the bowl. The petals will open to reveal your hidden message. *NOTE:* Do not get the paper flower wet before it is dropped into the bowl of water.

7. You can repeat the procedure to make flowers for others with whom you wish to share God's love. As you show them how to open the secret message, tell them about how God wants us to love one another.

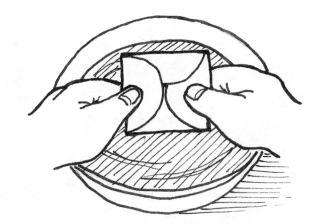

—— Memory Verse ——

Anyone who does not love does not know God, because God is love. (1 John 4:8)

—— Think about This ——

How do you show God's love to others?

47 Beauty Within

But the Lord said to Samuel, "Do not consider how handsome or tall he is. I have not chosen him. I do not look at the things people look at. Man looks at how someone appears on the outside. But I look at what is in the heart."—1 Samuel 16:7

Topic: Not judging people by how they look
Bible Exploration: 1 Corinthians 4:3; Romans 14:1–8

To **judge** is to decide if something is right or wrong. God wants you to judge some things, such as your actions. For example, when you are tempted to cheat in a game, you judge whether this would be right or wrong. But God doesn't want you to judge people by how they look.

In the Bible story about selecting a king for Israel, the prophet Samuel had one man in mind because of how he looked. But God didn't agree.

God made it clear that He is not concerned with appearance. God is concerned with what is in a person's heart. God doesn't judge by appearance, and He doesn't want us to, either.

In the following activity, black ink is used to demonstrate that what's inside a person may be very different from his or her outward appearance. Black ink is generally made of a mixture of different-colored particles. When these particles are mixed together, the ink looks black. When water moves through the paper, the different ink particles mix with the water and separate. The black ink has hidden colors inside it just as people have hidden beauty.

You Need   scissors
ruler
large, round coffee filter
transparent tape
pencil
1-quart (1-L) glass jar
black water-soluble marker (overhead
    projector pens work best)
tap water

1. Cut a 2-by-7-inch (5-by-17.5-cm) strip from the coffee filter.

2. Tape the end of the coffee filter strip to the pencil.

3. Lower the strip into the jar and support it by laying the pencil across the top of the jar. The paper strip should be relatively straight with its bottom edge touching the bottom of the jar. (If the strip is too long, shorten it by cutting off a section. If the strip is too short, repeat steps 1 and 2 using a longer strip or use a shorter jar.)

4. Remove the strip from the jar. Use the marker to draw a funny-looking cartoon character about 1 inch (2.5 cm) tall approximately 1 inch (2.5 cm) from the bottom of the paper strip.

5. Pour just enough water into the jar to cover its bottom. Then lower the strip into the jar, supporting the strip by laying the pencil across the top of the jar. The bottom of the strip should touch the water.

6. Observe the strip periodically for about 30 minutes.

7. Remove the strip from the jar. Cut across the top of the strip to remove it from the pencil. Allow the strip to dry and use it as a bookmark. The colorful bookmark will remind you that a person's outer appearance doesn't always reveal his or her inner beauty.

～ Memory Verse ～

Stop judging only by what you see. Judge correctly. (John 7:24)

～ Think about This ～

What does God want you to judge? How does God want you
to judge whether you will be friends with a person?

48 Smiley Face

I know what it's like not to have what I need. I also know what it's like to have more than I need. I have learned the secret of being content no matter what happens. I am content whether I am well fed or hungry. I am content whether I have more than enough or not enough.—Philippians 4:12

Topic: Be happy with what you have
Bible Exploration: Philippians 4:4, 10–13

Paul was in a filthy prison in Rome when the Holy Spirit directed him to write the letter that is now one of the books of the Bible called the Philippians. This letter was to a group of Christians in Philippi whom Paul had once visited. Paul knew and loved these people. You might expect Paul's letter to describe the horrible conditions of the prison and how sad Paul was. Instead it is a letter of joy and rejoicing.

At times during Paul's life, he had been wealthy and could have had anything he wanted. At other times, he had been hungry with no money to buy food; he had even been in prison. Paul explained this to his friends so that they would know he had learned to be content (satisfied) no matter what happened to him. Paul's contentment came from his faith, which was his trust and belief in Jesus. In his letter, Paul wrote that he could do anything by the power of Christ and that Christ gave him strength.

Paul's letter encouraged the Philippians to always think about things that are true, lovely, excellent, or worthy of praise. So if something happens that makes you sad, take the advice from this letter and find something happy to think about.

In the following activity, folding the paper changes a sad face to a smiley face. This is done by folding the paper in a certain way so that it causes the face on the paper to turn upside down. Remember that a smile is a frown turned upside down.

— UPSIDE DOWN —

You Need   sheet of white copy paper
   pencil
   crayons

1. Use the pencil to draw the face as shown on the next page.

2. Color the face with the crayons.

3. Lay the paper, sad face up, on a table.

4. Fold the paper in half two times, first from top to bottom, then from left to right.

6. Practice folding and unfolding the paper until you can quickly change the sad face to a smiley face. Show a friend that you can make the sad face change to a smiley face. If you work quickly, your friend may not see how you made the change. Challenge your friend to repeat the demonstration. You can share the secret folding and unfolding procedure with your friend if he or she cannot figure it out. And remember to think of good things and smile!

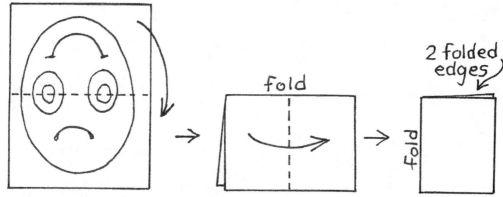

5. Lift the paper and unfold the bottom out to the left, then unfold the top half up.

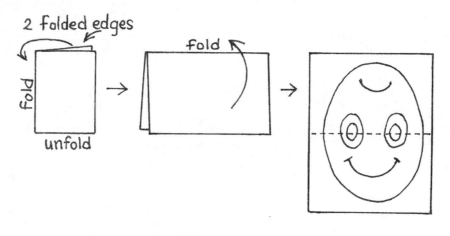

— Memory Verse —

A happy heart makes a face look cheerful. (Proverbs 15:13a)

— Think about This —

What makes you have a happy heart?
Are you happy with the things you have?

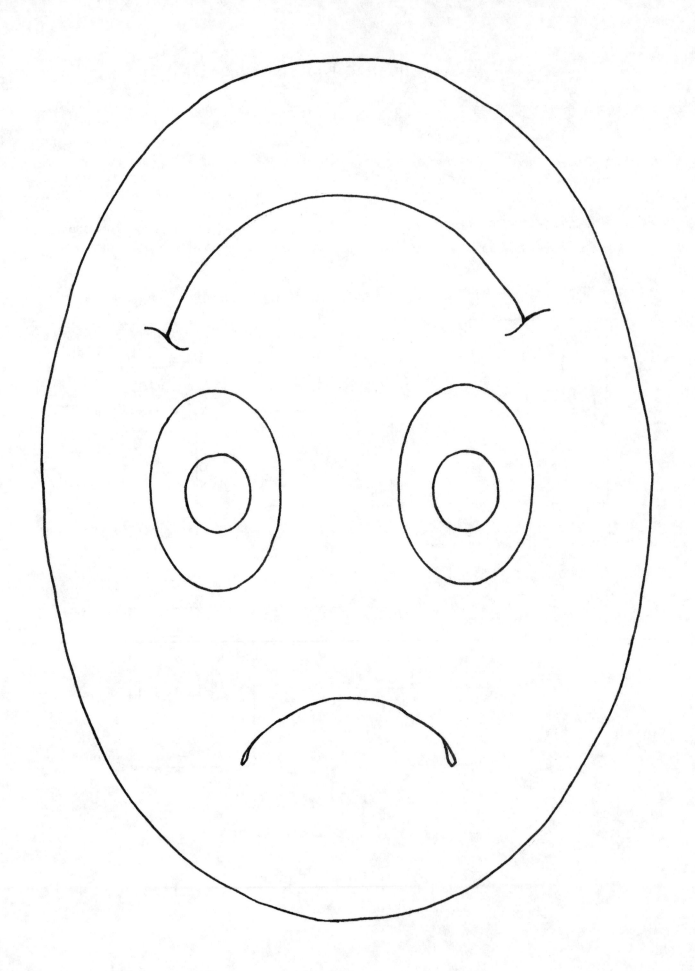

[49] Made by God

None of my bones was hidden from You when You made me inside my mother's body. That place was as dark as the deepest parts of the earth. When You were putting me together there, Your eyes saw my body even before it was formed. You planned how many days I would live. You wrote down the number of them in Your book before I had lived through even one of them.—Psalms 139:15–16

Topic: God has a plan for your life
Bible Exploration: Psalms 139:13–18

The Bible assures you that God purposely made you. It says that God knew you before you were even formed in your mother's body. You are important to God, and you should always remember that!

Even though you have two eyes, one nose, one mouth, and two ears, like everyone else, you are special and different from any other person. In fact, there are no two people on earth who are exactly the same. Even identical twins, who look alike, are not exactly alike.

In the following activity, fingerprints are used to demonstrate that you are special and one of a kind. A **fingerprint** is the special design of the ridges on your fingertips. The pattern of these ridges can be used to identify people, but their main job is to make it easier for you to pick up things. When you study your fingerprints and the fingerprints of others with a magnifying lens, you will find that there are basic fingerprint patterns. But close studies will reveal that all fingerprints are different.

You Need   pencil
2 sheets of white copy paper
transparent tape
magnifying lens

David

1. Rub the lead of the pencil back and forth across one of the sheets of paper.

2. Rub one fingertip across the pencil marking.

3. Cover the smudged fingertip with a piece of transparent tape. Press the tape firmly against your fingertip.

4. Carefully remove the tape and press the sticky side against the other sheet of paper.

5. Use the pencil to write your name underneath the fingerprint.

6. Use the magnifying lens to study the print. Compare your print to the basic fingerprint patterns.

7. Repeat steps 1 through 6, making prints of others. Fill the paper with prints.

8. You can put the title "Wonderfully Made" at the top of the paper and display it to remind you to pray for all the different people whose fingerprints are on the sheet. It will also remind you to thank God for making each of you so wonderfully different.

Basic Fingerprint Patterns

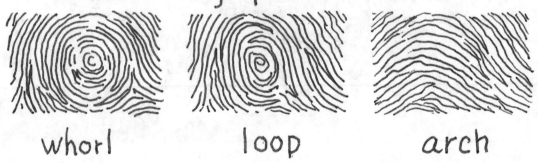

whorl   loop   arch

—— Memory Verse ——

*How You made me is amazing and wonderful.
I praise You for that. (Psalm 139:14a)*

—— Think about This ——

Your body is amazing. It lets you do all kinds of things,
but it needs your loving care for it to be healthy.
How can you keep your body healthy?

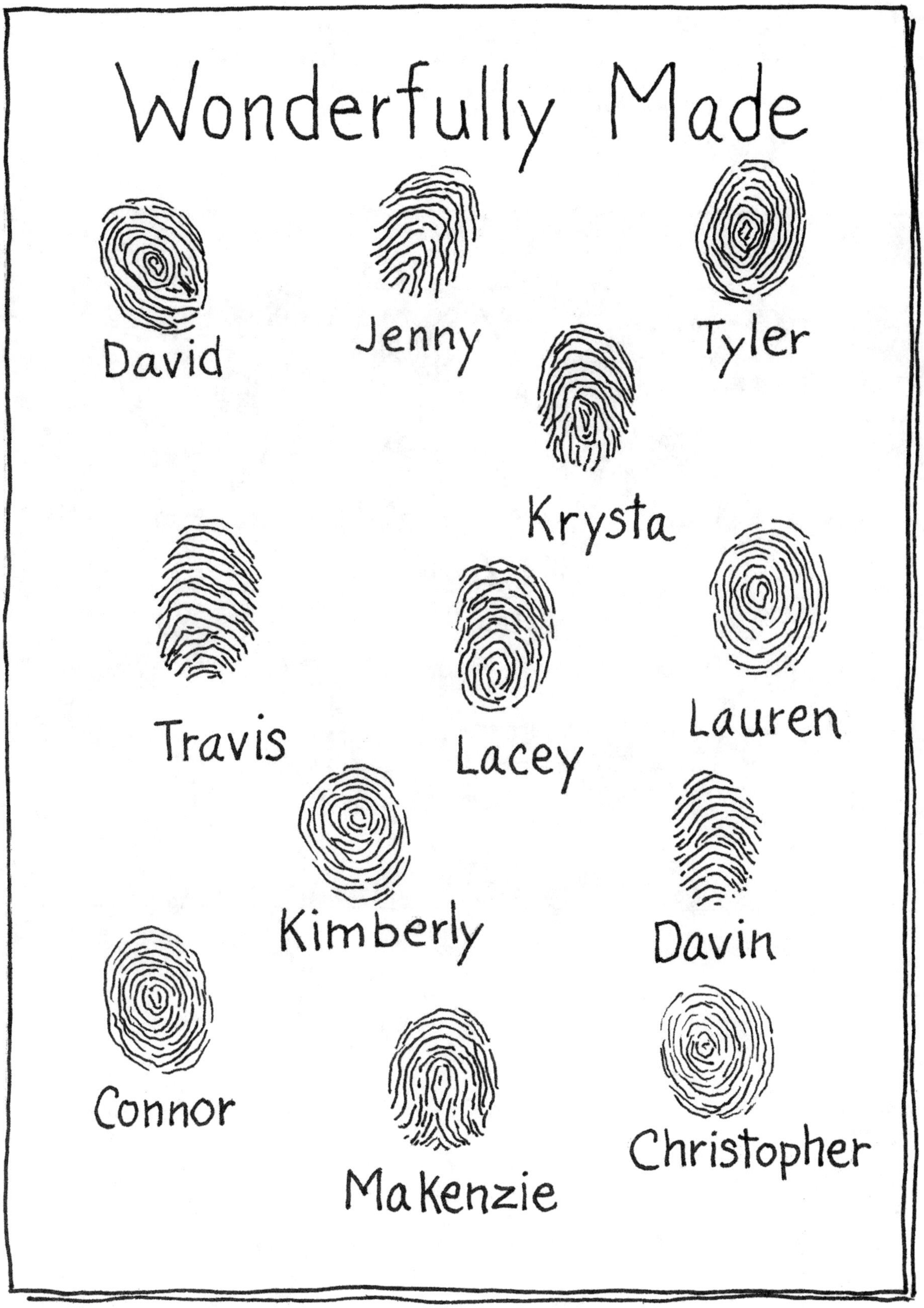

Wonderfully Made

David

Jenny

Tyler

Krysta

Travis

Lacey

Lauren

Kimberly

Davin

Connor

Makenzie

Christopher

50 Spreading Tales

Those who talk about others tell secrets. But those who can be trusted keep things to themselves.—Proverbs 11:13

Topic: Don't gossip

Bible Exploration: Proverbs 16:28, 20:19, 21:23; Luke 6:45; 2 Corinthians 12:20; James 3:1–5

To **gossip** is to talk about someone, especially to tell something that the person does not want others to know. There are different reasons for gossiping, including making yourself look better than the person being talked about or wanting to make someone look bad in the eyes of others. No matter what the reason, gossip hurts the person being talked about. The old saying "Sticks and stones may hurt my bones, but names will never hurt me" is not true. People are hurt and embarrassed when unkind things are said about them.

To resist the temptation of gossip, pray this prayer written by King David in Psalm 141:3: "Lord, guard my mouth. Keep watch over the door of my lips." The Holy Spirit will also help you resist the temptation not only to gossip but also to listen to gossip. One way He does this is to bring to your remembrance God's Word, which you have stored in your heart.

In the following activity, you will make a card as a reminder of how you can control your tongue and not gossip.

You Need   copy of Heart Pattern (see the
next page)
red crayon
scissors
ruler
pen
transparent tape

1. Make a photocopy of the Heart Pattern page.

2. Use the crayon to color the heart and verse strip red.

3. Cut around the outside of the pattern. Then cut out the box in the heart and the verse strip slot.

4. To make the paper fold more easily, use the ruler and the pen to draw back and forth across fold lines 1 and 2.

5. Fold the paper along fold line 1, then along fold line 2.

6. Secure tab A to section A with tape.

7. Insert the verse strip in the verse strip slot so that the verse is visible through the opening in the front of the card.

8. You can use the heart card to learn the verse on the card. You can make different verse strips by printing verses on strips of equal size.

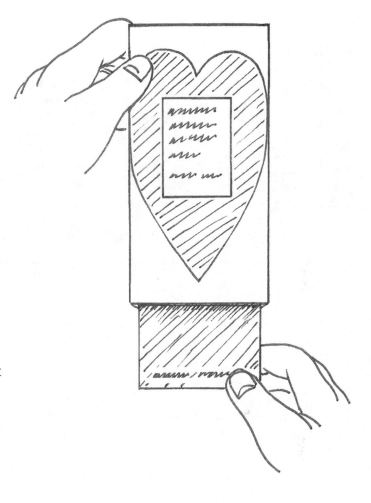

—— Memory Verse ——

Lord, may the words of my mouth and the thoughts of my heart be pleasing in Your eyes. (Psalm 19:14a)

—— Think about This ——

Do you listen to gossip? Do you gossip?
What can you do to not be tempted to
listen to gossip or to gossip yourself?

Heart Pattern

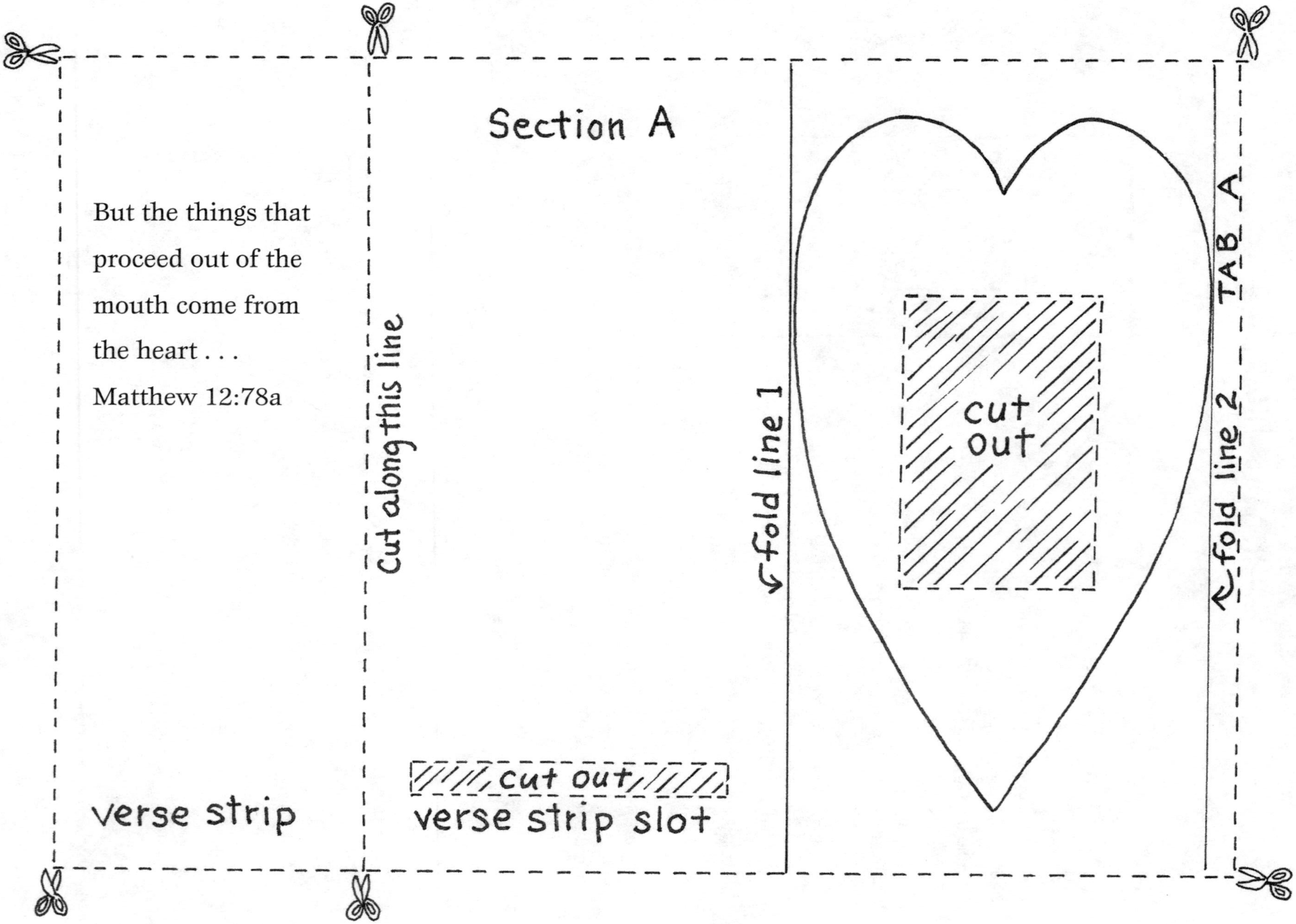

Section A

TAB A ↰Fold line 2

cut out

↰Fold line 1

Cut along this line

//cut out//
verse strip slot

But the things that
proceed out of the
mouth come from
the heart . . . .
Matthew 12:78a

verse strip

51 Friendship

No one has greater love than the one who gives his life for his friends.—John 15:13

Topic: You have a friend in Jesus
Bible Exploration: John 15:9–15

A friend is someone whom you can depend on. A friend likes being with you, makes you happy, is understanding when you make mistakes, encourages you, and is someone you can love and trust. Are you a good friend? If so, your friend can say all of these things about you.

If you disobey and break a rule at school, a good friend might agree to take the blame and be punished instead of you. However, this would be dishonest unless the teacher agreed to the switch. But you have a friend who has

already taken the punishment for any of God's rules that you might break during your whole life. This friend is Jesus, and God agreed to this switch. Jesus's punishment for your actions was death on the cross. Can you have a better friend than one who will die for you? Jesus is your very best friend. No one loves you as much as He does.

To know more about your friends at school or church, you spend time with them. You talk with them and share your thoughts. Jesus wants you to know more about Him. He wants you to spend time with Him, and He wants you to share your thoughts by praying. He will share

His thoughts through the words in the Bible. You can share Jesus with your friends by telling them about Him.

In the following activity, a balancing paper figure represents your need for Jesus in order to keep your life balanced. The figure represents what you can do on your own. Without paper clips, the paper figure does not balance. Instead it will fall. The two paper clips represent the help you receive from your friend Jesus. When the paper clips are added, the paper figure balances on your finger.

—— BALANCED ——

You Need copy of child (see below)
crayons
scissors
2 small paper clips

1. Make a photocopy of the child.

2. Use the crayons to color the child.

3. Cut out the child.

4. Extend one of your index fingers so it points out from your body.

5. Place the head of the child on the tip of your extended finger, then release the child. Note that it does not balance.

6. Clip one paper clip on the end of one of the hands. Move the clip so that it extends as far as possible past the edge of the hand. Repeat, placing the second paper clip on the other arm of the paper child.

7. With a paper clip on the end of each hand, repeat step 5. Note that with the two paper clips, the child balances on your finger. Remember that the paper clips represent the help you receive from your friend Jesus.

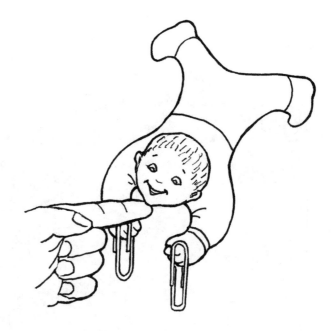

———— Memory Verse ————

A friend loves at all times. He is there to help when trouble comes.
(Proverbs 17:17)

———— Think about This ————

Who are your friends at school and/or church? Do they know about your very best friend, Jesus?

[52] The Good News

When I came to You, I was weak and afraid and trembling all over. I didn't preach my message with clever and compelling words. As I preached, the Holy Spirit showed His power. That was so You would believe not because of human wisdom but because of God's power. —1 Corinthians 2:3–5

Topic: Witnessing
Bible Exploration: 1 Corinthians 2:1–15

One of the books of the Bible, called Corinthians, is a letter that the Holy Spirit directed Paul to write to the Christians in Corinth. He describes his first visit to their church. He was there to tell them the truth of God's love. He had made up his mind that to do this he had to pay attention to only one thing, and that was Jesus Christ. He explains to the Corinthians that when he first preached at their church, he

was afraid and trembled all over. He didn't preach his message with clever or convincing words. But his listeners understood the message, not because of Paul's wisdom, but because of the power of the Holy Spirit.

Paul wanted the Corinthians to understand that they did not have to be trained speakers or to know everything about God's word. To be a witness for Jesus, they needed to **focus** (to direct their attention to one thing) on Jesus. If they would tell others the **Good News** that Jesus died for their sins and was raised from the dead so that they would have eternal life, then they could trust that the Holy Spirit would make the words of their message understandable. Christians today can also trust that the Holy Spirit will help them spread the Good News.

In the following activity, hidden letters remind you that to be a witness for Jesus, you need to focus on Him.

———— FOCUS ON JESUS————

Materials   copy of Jesus Name pattern (see the next page)
crayon or colored marker (use a dark color, such as red, blue, or green)
scissors
glue
sheet of colored construction paper
12-inch (30-cm) piece of string
transparent tape

1. Make a photocopy of the Jesus Name pattern page.

2. Use the crayon or marker to color within the lines outlining the striped shapes.

3. Cut around the outside of the rectangular figure.

4. Spread about a 1-inch (2.5-cm) strip of glue along the four sides of the paper, then lay the rectangle on the center of the construction paper.

5. Make a loop with the string. On the back of the construction paper, use tape to secure the ends of the string to the center of the top edge of the paper.

6. Using the string loop, hang the colored picture on the wall.

7. Stand in front of the colored picture about four steps away from the wall. Look at the picture. Do you see the letters formed by the shapes? You should see white letters that spell JESUS. If not, move back a couple of steps.

8. Leave the colored picture on the wall to remind you that, just like the picture, Jesus is always present. It will also remind you that sometimes we may be so busy with other things that we do not notice His presence. When we focus our eyes on Jesus, we can always find Him.

——— Memory Verse———

Pray also for me. Pray that when I open my mouth, the right words will be given to me. Then I can be bold as I tell the mystery of the good news. (Ephesians 6:19)

——— Think about This———

Are you afraid to tell others about Jesus because you don't know what to say? Have you prayed for boldness and the right words to say? Have you asked others to pray for you?

Jesus Name Pattern

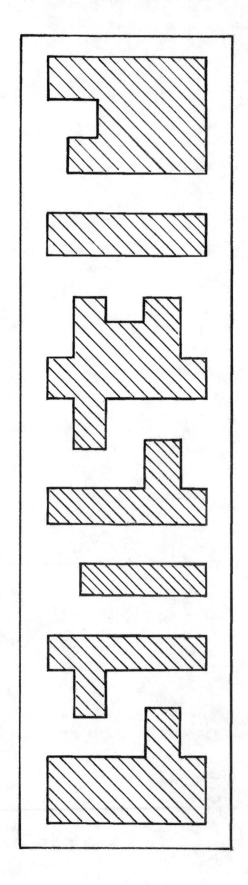

GLOSSARY

Abraham   A name that means father of many.

Abram   A name that means noble father.

acrostic   A list of words or phrases in which the first letter of each line forms a word.

activate   To put into action.

ark   A ship designed by God and built by Noah.

ark of the covenant   A large gold chest that held the stone tablets on which the Ten Commandments were written.

bad nature   A nature led by personal desires and that has no thoughts of pleasing God; sinful nature.

believers   Those who believe that Jesus died for their sins and rose from the dead so that we may have eternal life.

Bible   The Word of God made of 66 books: 39 in the Old Testament and 27 in the New Testament.

blessed   Rewarded by God.

children of Israel   See Israelites.

Christ   One of the names given to Jesus, meaning the Anointed One.

Christians   People who believe in Christ.

commandment   A rule made by God requiring a certain behavior; a law.

covenant   An agreement between people or between God and people.

create   To do something for the first time; God created everything in the universe out of nothing.

creation   Everything that exists; the universe.

deceived   Tricked.

devil   An enemy of God and people who tempts people to sin.

devoted   To be loyal and loving by giving your time, efforts, and attention.

disciple   A person who believes in Jesus; a Christian.

divine   Godly.

double-minded   Trying to be a slave to God and money at the same time.

Easter   A Christian holiday that marks the day when God raised Jesus from the dead. It is a day of thanksgiving for Jesus's sacrifice and a day of celebration for God's gift of eternal life.

eternal life   A new kind of life for believers. It is having fellowship with Jesus and help from the Holy Spirit now and being with and loved by God forever in heaven after you die.

eternity   Time without end.

faith   Trust and belief in God; trust in something or someone whom you believe is dependable.

faithful   Able to be trusted and depended on.

famine   A time when food is seriously scarce.

fast   To give up food for a while during a time of prayer and worship to God.

fingerprint   The special design of the ridges on a person's fingertips.

focus   To direct your attention to one thing.

follower   In reference to Jesus, it was someone who believes that Jesus is Lord; a disciple; a Christian.

forgive   To stop being angry at someone for what he or she has done.

fruit   The outward evidence of what is in our heart.

Garden of Eden   The beautiful garden prepared by God for Adam and Eve to live in.

gift   Something special given by one person to another.

God   The loving creator and ruler of the universe.

God's home   Where the children of God go to be with God forever after physical death; heaven.

good nature   A nature led by the Holy Spirit and that wants only to please God; spirit nature.

Good News   The fact that Jesus died for our sins and was raised from the dead so that we would have eternal life.

gossip To talk about someone, especially to tell something that the person doesn't want others to know.

grace God's love, kindness, and forgiveness shown to someone who has done nothing to deserve it.

heart In the Bible, it means the control center of all your thoughts and actions.

heaven (1) The sky. (2) God's home.

Hebrews See Israelites.

holy To be set apart for God. Belonging to God. Pure.

Immanuel A name for Jesus that means God is with us.

Israel (1) The name God gave to Jacob, Abraham's grandson. (2) The nation formed by the descendants of Jacob.

Israelites The descendants of Israel; also called the children of Israel, Hebrews, and Jews.

Jews Another name for the Israelites.

judge To decide if something is right or wrong.

law A rule made by God requiring a certain behavior; a commandment.

leprosy A disease that causes sores and can cause loss of feeling in the hands, feet, legs, and arms.

Lord A name for God that shows respect and means master or the one who is in control.

lost A description of a person who doesn't know that Jesus is his or her Savior.

manger A food box for animals.

Messiah A Hebrew word meaning the Anointed One.

miracle An amazing thing that only God can do.

nature Your behavior and thoughts.

parable A fictional story used to explain something.

Passover A yearly Jewish holiday that is a reminder of the last night the Israelites were slaves in Egypt, when the angel of death passed over the houses of those who followed the instructions that God gave to Moses.

pharoah A term for an Egyptian king.

physical death Death of the body.

plagues Things that cause widespread trouble and even death.

priestess A woman who directs worship services.

priests Men in charge of worship activities and holy things of the true God; men in charge of worship of false gods.

prophet A special person chosen by God to take His messages to people; a representative of a false god.

redeemed Ransomed; Jesus paid the penalty for our sins.

Redeemer The Son of God, the Lord Jesus.

sacrifice The killing of one thing in the place of another.

salvation Believing in God's saving grace.

saved A description of a person who knows that Jesus is his or her Savior.

sin Any action that displeases God; to disobey God such as by breaking His rules; doing what is wrong or not doing what is right according to God's rules.

sky The part of the universe surrounding Earth.

slave Someone who is controlled by something or someone.

sling A piece of leather used to throw small objects such as rocks.

spiritual death To be separated from the presence of God, the Source of Life.

spiritual food The Word of God, the Bible.

spiritual fruit The characteristics of a Christian's good nature: loving, joyful, peaceful, faithful, gentle, self-controlled, kind, good, and patient.

tempt To try to get someone to do something that is wrong.

tomb A cave in which people are buried.

trinity The three divine persons of God united into one divine being called God; God the Father, God the Son, and God the Holy Spirit.

vision A dream with a message from God.

waterproof Not letting water pass through.

wisdom An understanding that comes from God; the ability to make good decisions.

witness A person who tells what he or she has seen or knows; one who spreads the Good News.

worrying Being overly concerned about something.

worship To freely give love, honor, and praise.

INDEX